The Bulk Challenge Experience

The Bulk Challenge Experience

I. Ezax Smith

Published by Tablo

Table of Contents

REVIEW

The Bulk Challenge Experience is emotionally illuminating, intellectually constructed, and skillfully cataloged the carnage and terror when rival rebel groups besieged the Liberian capital Monrovia, on April 6, 1996. Indeed, it is a story in search of survival, and Ezax faced the options of getting murdered in Monrovia or fleeing on an overcrowded ship to Ghana. Ezax took one critical choice - to journey into the uncertainties in exile.

The Bulk Challenge Experience is a book of resilience that propelled Ezax to return home to a bleak future in Monrovia. It is a must-read, it is the story of endurance, and it is the testimony of resistance. Undeniably, the book is immensely enlightening and therapeutic.

Kai Gerald Wleh
Editor-In-Chief, African Star Newspaper

APPRAISAL

"I fled Liberia during the fracas of the April 6, 1996 warring fictions conflict in Monrovia because, in my mind, it was one of the most fearful moments of the Liberian Civil War. I have mentally overcome the occurrences of this episode, but I find it difficult to ignore or dismiss the memories of the journey on the Bulk Challenge.

Fleeing the danger ashore, the journey to safety became a nightmare at sea that threatened the survival of evacuees. Nights of torrential rainfall flooded and worsened the condition of the already ill-fated vessel. Fear of disaster heightened with every new day that we were rejected by neighboring countries. But as fearful and uncertain as the entire journey was, our faith in God to see us through increased even more – day after day.

This Book captures the shared experiences of real people including me, whose lives have forever been imparted by that frightful journey. Ezax is an excellent communicator and a master recorder of chronological events. It is a good read with real life lessons recommended for all ages. He has captured the experiences of this voyage like none other could, and I hope you will find the story as intriguing as it is to me."

LT Solomon O. Lloyd, CHC, USN.
US Marine Corps/California, USA

DEDICATION

This book is dedicated to all peoples of the world who experience calamities, natural disasters, differences and diversities; and, particularly, to the people I refer to as "The CHALLENGERS"—the men, women, boys, girls, children, and the elderly—who survived the horrific 10-day sail from Liberia to Ghana, on the ill-fated Nigerian vessel, *Bulk Challenge*. The spirit of unity and selfless love exhibited on that dreadful journey will forever be a reminder that as Liberians, and as people in our common world – in spite of our differences – we can be better; that we can work together to reach the dreams we've always held for ourselves and our countries; and make the world a better place.

ACKNOWLEDGEMENT

Writing this book took some time and intentional effort, and I am thankful to God for the endurance He gave me to see it to the end. During this process, I have had to compare notes with few fellow travelers. In addition, I have had to use specific names of others. For these various groups and individuals, I'm forever grateful.

For reading earlier manuscripts of this book and offering important suggestions, I would like to thank my friend, Timothy Lincoln Reeves, Sr.; for providing a professional touch of editorial and structural content to the final manuscript, I am grateful to Prof. Dr. K. Moses Nagbe; and for writing the forward to this book, I am thankful to my friend, Professor Welma Mashinini Redd.

Furthermore, I like to thank Ms. Sherae Davis for sketching the original interior graphic illustrations, and Pradip Chakraborty for the final interior graphics and book cover illustrations. To a special group of people, I call the "enabler" – your moral, spiritual and other support to the completion of this project is highly appreciated. You helped put this book in the hands of readers. Thanks to Solomon O. Lloyd, Josephine Hutchinson, Satta Grice-Nyemah, Julius Goundor, Lydia & Lavie Smith, Annabea Paegar, Jonathan Mason, Abraham H. Teah, Calvin Freeman, James Lee and Tommy Sharrow.

To Eric Weah Collins, Kadiatu Konteh-Borajhi, Charles Tieh Bropleh, Rev. Dr. J. Edwin Lloyd, Sr., Alston Wolo, Feona Johnson-Togba, Prince Jallabah, Claudia Spiller-Jargbah, Dr. Pearl Banks-Williams, Mr. & Mrs. Sam Weedor, Karmanieh Charlene Reeves,

Theophylus During, II, C. Wallace Williams, Grant Martin, Fatu Barduae, Doctor Michel Dioubate and Hon. Gayah Fahnbulleh, I thank you for joyfully accepting my invite to participate in the sharing of your experiences. By this, you validate the story of the Bulk Challenge Experience, and I am grateful.

This book would not have been completed without the support of my family who allowed me the privacy to think and write – especially my grand-son, Lemel Samukai, who spent many nights with me in the basement, while I worked on the materials for my manuscript, and to my grand-daughter, Mandisa Bestman, for keeping me company while I worked. Thank you all very much.

Finally, I would like to thank my publisher for accepting to publish my work. And to all of you who are reading through these pages, I thank you and welcome you to journey with us.

GLOSSARY

"Across the Bridge" - all areas beyond the two bridges that connect to the City of Monrovia.

Bazzam — a local Liberian term for a type of fabric used for clothing.

Banku — a part of Ghanaian diet prepared from fermented corn. It is also processed and eaten with a variety of soups.

Charlie – a common name referred to any male. Whether the name a known or unknown, many Ghanaians calls all men, *Charlie*.

Chop Bar — a Ghanaian term for makeshift spots at street corners where cheap food is sold.

Cook Shop — a Liberian term for makeshift spots where cheap food is sold.

Five-Fingers — a kind of plant that looks like the leaves of potatoes grown in Liberia. The plant grows as wild vines in bushes in many places around the country. It had not been eaten as food prior to the Liberian civil war. However, when food became very scarce, risk-takers began experimenting with the plant. Soon, many more people began cutting and cooking "five-fingers," which derived its name from being shaped like the human hand when opened with fingers spread.

Fula Bread – a long bread made in several sizes: 6 inches or 12 inches long, and sometimes, 24 inches. It got its name from the Fulanis from Guinea residing in Liberia, and who known for making them.

Fufu — a part of West African diet prepared from cassava tubers. It is often gritted, stored in bags until it ferments. And it is processed and eaten with a variety of soups.

Grad — Ghanaian local use of the word "glad."

Lappa — a local Liberian term for wrapping cloth. The term may be used to make generic reference to any fabric for clothing.

Okaaay — suggests a response of uncertainty. When a Ghanaian is not sure of some information, he/she usually begins with the word "Okaaay." Anyone accustomed to that will make a tacit acceptance of the response. For example, if you ask, "Where can I find the ABC Store?" Answer: "Okaaay, if you go this way and turn left, it will be right there to your left." Perhaps, the desire to simply offer an answer is the sign that Ghanaians generally do not want to disappoint. They apparently do not know how to say "I don't know."

Palm Cabbage — a Liberian dish prepared from the buds of oil palm and coconut trees. Harvesting such a bud leads to the death of the tree. During the Liberian civil war, many oil palm and coconut trees were destroyed in that way. But with the scarcity of food, scavenging for palm cabbage became inevitable. In that process, oil palm and coconut trees, which normally have more economic and health values in terms of fresh air, shade, oil, brooms, etc., were destroyed.

Par – a local Ghanaian expression which suggests that something is far away.

Prace — Ghanaian local use of the word "place."

Shake-hand – a local Liberian term, which may suggest the sign of making peace in order to put behind some dispute. It may also refer to a sign of bribery. If someone says "you've got to shake my hand," it may be another way of requesting a bribe. In this situation, what may make it less of a pressure is that the amount will have to be at the giver's discretion. What the giver does simply is to put the amount in the recipient's pocket.

Stole-way – to steal your way is to forcefully and or illegally enter an area, event or activity without permission.

This-thing — a Ghanaian generic reference to anything. The term "this-thing" flies from a Ghanaian who cannot think readily of the name of something being referred to. For example, "I want you to give me the "this-thing." That could be a chair, a book, cup or whatever.

"Town trap is not for rat alone" — a philosophical punch line derived from one of numerous folktales of Liberia's indigenous population. The expression is often made to those who may ignore the need to build collective defense against external threats. It was popularized when the Liberian leader Samuel Doe, in the early months of the Liberian civil war, used it to invite a collective Liberian resolve against the invading forces of Charles Taylor and other warlords.

Wachen — a name of Kwa origin. Kwa is an African linguistic group. In Liberia, this group comprises of Bassa, Grebo and Kru. Wachen means heart-breaker.

FOREWORD

Challenges of survival that Ezax Smith and others faced as a result of the Liberian civil war brought out the best in people who already had fine character traits. Ezax' innate nature as a humanitarian, a leader and an organizer, helped people who had all but lost hope. He awakened the human spirit on that trip, as he also did in the Liberian community in Baltimore, and among Liberians across the Americas. His gift for bringing people together for the good of the whole shines brightly, especially in his spiritual life. To Ezax, I say: "Thank you for the tireless hours of community service and especially for capturing this part of Liberia's history, which really needs to be preserved and shared with future generations and the world."

The Bulk Challenge Experience reminds us that caring for each other, helping each other and working for the good of each other—all demonstrations of love—are the only actions that can make our nation, or any nation recovering from disaster, whole again.

Welma Campbell Mashinini Redd
Assistant Professor of Film & Broadcasting
Morgan State University
Baltimore, Maryland

PRELUDE

Years later, the memory of the experience is still as fresh as if it happened just yesterday. I walked to the front of the deck to go down and share the news of the reassurance from the captain, that we would make the trip, or, at worst, be reimbursed. To my dismay, the ship was slowly drifting from the dock. I could hear the shouts of thousands of prospective passengers who were standing in the port yard, waiting, just as I was, for their names to be called. I looked and saw my wife standing nearby. I was tempted to jump over board, but the space between the boat and the dock had now widened, and I would have fallen into the ocean or hit my head on the wall of the concrete dock had I tried jumping. Without mention, my wife ran a little closer, food in one hand and a large bottle of water in the other. She had reasoned that if I stayed on board, I would need food for at least three days of journey. She threw the food over into the ship and bid me well. "Make sure you get our things when you get there," she shouted.

"This cannot be happening," I thought for a moment. All arrangements had been made; I had tickets in my hands, and had spoken twice with the captain who assured me we would board before the end of the day. But as the day sped by, what appeared to be broad-day corruption was happening before our very eyes. It was becoming obvious that we would not make it into the boat; for hundreds of individuals who had not followed the process to register officially or pay for their tickets were bribing soldiers who were manning the entrance to the ship. I mean, these hundreds of individuals were entering while we who held legitimate tickets waited to be called on board. Several hundreds of those who paid bribes entered illegally on the ship, and it seemed already full to overflowing. Furious about the situation, I decided I would go on board to meet the captain for the third time. I wanted to know what the situation was with the illegal entering of passengers while legitimate ticketholders were standing on line. But perhaps, I forgot that this, too, was Africa; and more so, we were in a war situation, which many unscrupulous individuals were shamelessly taking advantage of. I made my way to the side entrance but was soon stopped by two soldiers who asked me to pay before I entered. "Anything you got will do," one of them said to me in that husky and heavy Nigerian accent. I showed my ticket and receipt and insisted to see the captain. Both soldiers refused and proceeded to hit me with a rubber coil they used to beat people off the ship. A senior officer on board saw the commotion and hailed them to allow me to speak with him. I went on board and informed him of my prior two meetings with the captain and his instruction to see him whenever I had a problem. The captain was fond of me. We have met and spoken on many occasions. I had registered a total of 14 people including cousins and friends with whom my family and friends pooled funds to make the process easier. From an economic standpoint, I had boosted their coffers at one shot. "Mr. Smith, we will take care of you and your family, not to worry," he had assured me earlier.

I made my way to the captain's cabin along with a few other individuals who has similar concerns. It was difficult getting through because of the many people who had illegally entered the ship and the many others who were already there, requesting reimbursement because they did not see the possibility of getting on board with their families. By the time I spoke with the captain and headed back through the crowd, the ship crew had decided to leave because they determined that the ship was overloaded, even though hundreds of ticketholders were still standing in line in the dockyard.

And so it was! I was heading to Ghana on the vessel named Bulk Challenge; or so I thought.

This is the account of the incredible 10-day journey on the Atlantic Ocean aboard this leaking ship, Bulk Challenge; the experiences of the challenges faced, lessons learned, and life beyond the journey.

THE APRIL 6, 1996 FRACAS

It had never been our plan to leave the country. We had survived seven years of the civil war, although under strenuous circumstances. We fled every intense fighting area and managed to move the family each time into a safer place. Nowhere is safe in a civil war situation, but with God on one's side, he makes a way each time it seems unfeasible. This is how I know that God is real and in control of human destiny. To think the power of God is unreal is to believe that you can live without breathing. In the case of my family, the idea of constantly moving from place to place, particularly with two young children, was becoming unbearable and dangerous, to say the least.

Fierce fighting resumed between warring factions on April 6th, when the National Patriotic Front of Liberia (NPFL) and United Liberation Movement, the Kromah faction, (ULIMO-K) wedded and attempted to arrest the leader of the ULIMO, the Johnson faction, Mr. Roosevelt Johnson. It was seemingly one of the dumbest ideas because all factions were serving within the same locality and on the Transitional Council—the 5-man leadership team comprising heads of the various fighting forces. That decision to arrest Johnson sparked the renewed fighting and ignited a new and intense wave of fear. Once again, Liberians in central Monrovia were awakened to the sound of sporadic gun fires, so loud it could blow your ear drums out. The guns sounded like RPG, GMG, AK47 and M1—all together. We'd heard them before and were familiar with those sounds. In fact, many Liberians were. Yet, each time those sounds re-surged, they sent fear down many spines.

The shooting seemed so close as if at the back of our house. Looking outside, I saw people in large numbers with sacks, bulging pillow cases, suitcases, and even empty rice bags stuffed with different items. These people were heading toward one of the main streets in the community. The scene was reminiscent of the early days of the crisis when hundreds of thousands of people fled their homes in fear of reprisals from misguided government soldiers or the so-called freedom fighters (rebels). I needed no confirmation that the fighting was nearing our neighborhood. I called out to my wife to gather the children, while I bundled some clothes and food to take on the journey.

"How long," was anybody's guess. It could be for a day or two, a week or even longer, depending on the intensity of the fighting and the occupancy of the neighborhood by armed men. Which fighting force occupying an area is essential to the decision one made to return or remain out of that area. Our children were very young, and all they had known so far were sounds of guns, and running and hiding from stray bullets. I couldn't imagine what was running through their young minds, but I figure they were quite aware that we were in some bad times, and bad people were moving about to hurt some good people. We had discussed with them earlier, regarding the war and the fact that we would have to move constantly in order to stay alive and protect them from harm. They understood that we loved them much, not to want anything harmful happening to them. Looking back, I think talking with our kids about the war and what to expect and do in difficult times helped them cooperate in the manner they did.

Our children, Lydia was 5 and Ismad, 4, when the war began in 1990. Lavie was born in the heat of the war, that same year when the curfew was set at 6pm to 6am daily. My wife was nine months pregnant and due to give birth any moment. Each day we would pray that she did not go into labor at night but rather during the daytime when we could move about and get to the nearest hospital. This was important because we had heard of people out in the street, being shot—regardless of why they were out. There was even a rumor that a pregnant woman was shot as she made her way to the hospital. True or false, we had seen much, heard much, and knew much that anything was possible, and there was no time to take chances.

Thankfully, one day my wife got into labor in broad daylight—at exactly 3:15pm in the afternoon, and we had ample time to get to the hospital and get back home before curfew. In Monrovia, our nation's capital, we lived on 9th Street, Sinkor, at the time, down Coleman Avenue. Just a walking distance away from our home—two blocks away—at the corner of 9th Street and Russell Avenue, was the Subah Clinic. Mrs. Lusu Subah was a well know Midwife at the J. F. Kennedy Maternity Center, and had a private practice attached to her home. That was where we went, and what a joy it was to bring home a baby girl who did not ask to come in this world at the time, and who knew nothing whatsoever that was happening. We named her "Lavie"—from la vie, the French word meaning "life." Her traditional Bassa name became "Tomah"— meaning, "War Woman or Woman of War." Then just two weeks after her birth, our community was bombed and we were in the streets fleeing for our lives again.

Every time I think about that fateful day, I remember how stupid I was for earlier refusing to leave the community with my baby. I was so mad with the foolishness that I told my father and family to go and leave me in the house; that I was not taking my young two-week old baby in the open air with bullets flying about. But wisdom prevailed that day when my father asked me to leave. I obeyed him and left. With my baby girl in my arms, we walked to the main street and joined the multitude of movers who were going nowhere particular. We just wanted to get out of the community. No one knew what was going on; houses were hit by rockets, people were killed; and as I made my way from the house, I passed by a 9-year-old girl whose entire leg was severed by fragments from a rocket. She was lying in a pool of blood on the side of the street, and there was nothing we could do. A friend of ours was asleep in her room when her house was hit with fragments from a rocket; she was killed instantly.

We walked up to Tubman Boulevard and joined the crowd going toward Sinkor. It was later that we got to know what had happened. The rumor was that rebels had entered the community by way of the Duo River. The soldiers were instructed to fire rockets in the direction of the Duo River, but they had instead aimed them in the direction of the community. The soldier who fired one of the rockets was the son of the Jarbahs, a prominent family in our community. When he looked through the binoculars he had, he observed that the instrument was pointing in the direction of our community. According to him, he tried to convince the soldiers that he lived in that community and that no rebels were there, but they were not paying him any mind and insisted that he fired it anyhow. Because he was not a member of the ruling tribe (Krahn), he could not argue much or else he would have been charged or labeled an enemy of the Doe-led Government or one working against the effort of the army. As he aimed the barrels in the direction of the community, he tried to tilt it away but couldn't get it far away enough without someone observing his move. So he fired it right into the community. "It would have been worse," he said, had he not tilted it away, but the devastation was still agonizing.

So, here we were, walking away from danger, fleeing from the horror in the community, an action that was reported to President Doe that we were protesting in the streets. See how things can get twisted so easily under these circumstances? Well, without investigation, a battalion was sent out with the instruction to get rid of the protestors in the streets. It happened that Jackson Doe, a cousin of the President, was in route to the Executive Mansion when he met the crowd around 18th Street, Sinkor. He was one of the few respected government officials in the Doe-led government. He inquired about why we were in the streets in such mass number. "What is going on?" he asked. It was explained to him that we were just getting out of the area, fleeing from the rain of bullets and rockets on our community. He cautioned the group to get off the main street and be mindful as such mass movement could be misinterpreted. No sooner after he left the group, we learned he intercepted a battalion from the Executive Mansion. They recognized him and accorded him the necessary military courtesy before continuing with their mission. He asked about their mission and they explained that they were sent to get rid of the protestors in the streets. For clarity, *get rid of* meant *to kill*. In other words, the soldiers were sent to kill all the people in the streets because information had reached some military authorities that the people were protesting against the government. Those people in the streets included me and my family. But Jackson Doe saved our lives when he sent them back after clarifying that we were not in the streets to protest but rather fleeing for our lives. Had the soldiers come before he came by, it would have meant a massacre and this story would not have been told.

That was just one of those crazy episodes we experienced in the early days of the Liberia civil war. That was then. Several years had gone by now and although the war raged on, there were periods when the violence subsided and children were back in school, beginning to be normal again—doing children things. Our daughter was now five years old, approaching six, and all of a sudden April 6th was upon us, halting activities of daily living again, after we had struggled to reconstruct them. This was a vexing pattern that left the war-affected people feeling disheartened and hopeless.

Moving and running from place to place was a daunting experience, particularly for little children who were being robbed of the opportunity to be children—to grow and play in communities like children would. As the war dragged on, schools were disrupted so very often that many children lost the interest, motivation and passion for school. As a result, many families had to take on the responsibility to educate their children during periods of closures. In that way, if or whenever schools re-opened the children would be prepared to continue at their pre-war level.

"Where are we going Daddy?" asked our young daughter. How hard it was to explain to a six-year-old that we had to just leave so nobody got hurt! I am not sure she understood, but she went along. At least she was smart enough not to ask the "why," "why," "why" questions that children that age often ask.

So, on that April day in 1996, I grabbed what little I could: mainly food stuff and bits of changing clothes. "When the fighting stops, we will return home," I reassured my family. We stepped out, and by this time, almost the entire community was heading toward the ELWA Red Light, a major intersection that leads either westward to the city center of Monrovia or eastward outside Paynesville toward Kakata, in Margibi County. We joined the crowd heading nowhere particular. There was no set place in mind to take my family. As we walked, I thought about all the possible places we could stop, to rest or stay at night. The names of close friends came to mind but I wasn't sure if they would be home since we had not seen them in months. At this point, we just wanted to get out of the danger zone and into a safer area.

On my head was a half bag of rice (Liberia's staple), and in my hands were two motley striped bags, which Liberians often refer to as 'refugee bags', stacked with clothes and other basic necessities. My wife had the 6-year-old on her back and the 11- year-old clung to her right arm.

"We approached the 'Junction' and joined the larger crowd heading west toward the Red Light area.
It was apparent we could not go West toward the city, so we just kept going with the crowd"

We headed away from the sounds of the bullets toward the
ELWA intersection often referred to simply as the "Junction."
ELWA -Eternal Love Winning Africa - had long become a
community, from which an interdenominational Christian
group had established a strong media presence, airing news
and religious teachings. The idea of running under bullets time
after time was becoming increasingly frustrating. As we
approached the "Junction" we observed a much larger crowd
heading Northeast toward the Red Light area. It was apparent we
could not go West toward the city, so we just kept going with
the crowd. The mass movement was a result of fear—fear of
being caught between warring forces; fear of becoming
casualties, as it often was the fate of the civilian population when
fighting erupted in an area.

Experiences showed that it was not wise to remain in any area
when fighting forces met, except you were a military person and
had weapons for self-protection. It was still not safe to have your
family and little children in those situations, even if you were a
military person. And so, at the sound of excessive shootouts—no
ordinary shooting—it made good sense to get away before it was
too late. The word on the street was that it was Government
forces—the Armed Forces of Liberia (AFL) — advancing from town
in an attempt to stop the rebel forces from reaching the city center.
This news was confusing to many of us, more so because no one
could understand who AFL were referring to as "rebels" when in
fact, all of the factional rebel forces were represented in
government and within the city. But as with any rebel war, there is
no time for reasoning; whatever the AFL meant was good enough
for us to get away from the center of any gunfight.

Two hours on the journey and after several miles of walking,
we encountered a friend of ours— Cedrick Reeves—with his
family. The Reeves had also vacated their home and were looking
for safety. It was a joy to see Cedrick. It had been a while since we
met. We had known one another since high school, in the early
1980s. Our acquaintance was strengthened when we found
ourselves part of the same church. Both of us loved to sing and

were members of the church's Junior Choir. Cedrick was a lead vocalist and sang first tenor. As for me, I sang second tenor and later bass. We grew up as young adults in the church, learning and participating in numerous church and church-related activities. Over time, we related to each other more like brothers than mere friends. Cedrick's wife Nora was also a member of the choir, just as my wife was. We were just one big family!

Occasionally during the war, we would meet and share our experiences and challenges. Interestingly, we kept jobs—whatever there was—and we were thankful that God continued to sustain us. Sometimes we filled each other's needs, such as food, money and basic necessities. On this day of seeking a place of safety, we walked and talked about our disappointments and the disruptions and the constant uprooting that the war was causing families; the unbearable mental and physical strain and stress that it brought on us.

We reflected on how it was easier to get around by oneself, but how extremely difficult it was when one had to look out for the welfare and safety of others. So was the situation with family men like Cedrick and myself and many others like us. Within the war, we fought a different kind of fight. Ours was not the bullets and gun types, but the type that challenged us to fetch for food, ensure protection of family from heartless men and women, and secure a safe place when night finally came and the family could rest from hurdles of the day.

As we continued the journey that day, Nora, Cedrick's wife, informed us that she had a sister or cousin who lived near the Freeport. However, she was not sure whether the person was home or had traveled. They would stop by anyway, once they got to the Freeport. Nora asked if we would like to join them. Of course, you know what my answer was: a resounding "YES." I said it so fast, we all laughed about it; but the truth was, I wanted to be the first to say "yes" before someone walking behind or beside us answered – thinking he/she was being spoken to. Funny enough, no one else was traveling that close to us. Anxiety has a way of creating needless suspicion. Anyway, hearing and feeling the eagerness in my voice, Nora couldn't help laughing: "You are so crazy!" she said and we laughed the thought away.

Those who know me well, know that I can be very humorous sometimes. I make little jokes here and there regardless of the situation. It worked for me; it takes away some of the stress, ease the tension and keeps me going to the next mile. We started singing some choruses along the way; it seemed to have shortened the distance. A good song in trouble times can sure make a difference in how you receive and deal with the circumstance—particularly, when you internalize the message or words of the song in relation to your current situation. Think about such songs like "You are God/ You never change. / We bow to you, / We exalt your name", or "Jesus Never Fail Me Yet", or "God Has an Army Marching through the Land", or "In Moments like These", or "I Know the Lord Will Make a Way for Me." As you can see, these songs bear so much promise and inspiration that just believing them as you sing can help strengthen your psyche. True gospel singing is preaching through music. It is a powerful way of reawakening your spirit and inspiring a zeal that increases your faith. And that was exactly what these choruses did to us. It calmed our fears and increased our faith in knowing that we would make it through and that God was walking with us.

For most of us who grew up in the church, and particularly in the choir, music has always been a source of comfort and relief in our down moments. When you feel all alone and weary; when you think your world is falling in on you; when friends, families and foes forsake you; and you have no one to turn to, just begin to sing and meditate on the words of a song—a gospel song or hymn. Soon, you will begin to see the problem from a whole different perspective. So, my family and Cedrick Reeves' family walked and sang and laughed and talked, and looked out for the kids, as we journeyed on.

By the time of the April 6th outbreak of hostilities, it had been almost seven years since the war began and still there seemed to be no resolution in sight. Peace accords and attempts by the international community and other mediation groups to resolve the conflict had failed time after time. From the outset of the conflict, the African sub regional body, the Economic Community of West African States (ECOWAS), undertook several initiatives to bring about a peaceful settlement. Its efforts were supported by the United Nations. The efforts included establishing, in 1990, an ECOWAS observer force, the Economic Community Military Observer Group (ECOMOG). Ceasefires after ceasefires were broken over the years.

In 1992, a Special Representative was appointed by the Secretary General of the United Nations to assist in talks between ECOWAS and the warring factions. By 1996, about ten peace agreements or accords had been signed and broken by parties to the conflict: The Banjul III Agreement, October 24, 1990; the Bamako Ceasefire Agreement, November, 1990; the Banjul IV Agreement, December, 1990; the Lomé Agreement, February, 1991; the Yamoussoukro IV Peace Agreement, October, 1991; and the Geneva Agreement, April, 1992[1]. The Cotonou Accord was brokered in 1993 by ECOWAS in Cotonou, Benin. Soon after, the United Nations Security Council established the United National Observer Mission in Liberia (UNIMIL), to support ECOMOG in implementing the Cotonou Peace Agreement, particularly, as regards compliance by all parties[2]. UNIMIL was the first United Nations peacekeeping mission undertaken in cooperation with the West African peacekeeping initiative. And yet, by May 1994, renewed fighting broke out, rendering the Cotonuo Agreement another failure.

By this same time, the United Liberation Movement of Liberia for Democracy (ULIMO) had disintegrated into two militia groups: ULIMO-J, a Krahn faction led by Roosevelt Johnson and ULIMO-K, a Mandingo faction under Alhaji G.V. Kromah. With the emergence of new factions, the security situation in Liberia became more and more volatile.

There were now approximately seven factional groups including the Armed Forces of Liberia, the National Patriotic Front of Liberia (NPFL), the Independent National Patriotic Front of Liberia (INPFL), ULIMO-J, ULIMO-K, the Liberia Peace Council (LPC) and the Lofa Defense Force (LDF). Apparently, everybody was fighting everybody. This became the crux of the fear: everyone was perceived as an enemy by the numerous fighting forces. If you fled from fighting into an area, you were still not safe because you would seem strange to someone, and because of the self-evident fear and uncertainty, you could be killed without questions, on grounds that you were an enemy. No wonder Liberians evacuated into exile in mass numbers. Indeed, no one was safe anymore in a land once known as one of the safest, more peaceful and hospitable places in Africa. Liberia was now a "dog-eat-dog" land, where, as Liberians often say, "everybody for himself, and God for all." To live and survive under these circumstances had to be by the protection of a higher being, and for some of us, that being was God. He shields his own and provides passage for them even in the midst of the most dangerous situations. It had to be God.

By September 1994, factional leaders agreed to another ceasefire in Ghana. That agreement became known as to the Akosombo Peace Accord[3], which was intended obviously to stop the fighting and encourage the establishing of a democratically elected government. But that agreement yielded little effect. The warring factions continued to fight, demonstrating unwillingness to honor the agreement. There were occasional and sometimes extended shoot-outs among the various groups. Ceasefire was just a word not put into action. Pockets of shootings and fights continued until December 1994, when factions and parties signed what came to be known as the Akosombo Clarification. Notwithstanding the clarification, fighting continued.

There seemed to be a purpose far greater than the claim of

factional leaders: to rescue the Liberian people. Each agreement seemed to have all the ingredients for peace, yet factional leaders reneged on every commitment to resolve the conflict. Each time, these factional leaders trumped up reasons, claiming that the agreements did not go far enough to ensure the interest and benefit of the Liberian people. However, critics began to see that the motives of these factional leaders were more personal and deeply rooted in greed for power and money. This glaring evidence of selfishness created skepticism in the minds of many as to whether there was any intention for peace on the part of any of the leaders. Unfortunately, in such matters of uncompromising greed of fighting forces, it is the common people who become the ultimate victims.

So, when on August 19, 1995 it was announced that the warlords had agreed to another accord called the Abuja Peace Accord[4], the confidence of ordinary people in warring factions had worn thin. There was little hope that it would last, and justly so! Regardless of the Abuja Accord, fighting broke out again in April 1996. Once again, the fear of death was in the air, and here we were, in the streets—Cedrick, I, our families and untold number of other families—headed to nowhere.

Cedrick's family and mine made several stops along the way, meanly because of the children who were tired, wanted to rest, drink or ease themselves. At one of our stops at the back of the Paynesville Town Hall, one of the children inquired about where we would spend the night. There was sporadic shooting everywhere and we couldn't continue for a moment. Vehicles were zooming by in speeds as if in a race; they were avoiding the main roadway. The occupants of some of the vehicles, we observed, were relatives of officials of the government--particularly, from the NPFL group. There was no mistaking they themselves were trying to get away. This rush suggested the level of the seriousness of the situation. Because these relatives were close to those in power, it was assumed that they knew something that we did not know—perhaps, how serious this fight was getting, or how uncontrollable it could get.

With such scenes playing out, we, the ordinary "get-aways" became even more frightened. We had seen many people die before our very eyes, shot in front of us, or gutted out as we walked by—so much so that dying was not dreaded but expected any day. Such was our predicament, the frustration of constantly being in harm's way, that at some point during the journey I decided we would head to the Freeport of Monrovia to check on the possibility of any passenger ship or boat that was preparing to evacuate residents out of the country. Cedrick had the same thought and so we planned to support one another during these times.

As a matter of fact, hundreds of people were headed to the Freeport. Apart from it being an outlet, it was perhaps one of the safest places in the city because it was the official base of ECOMOG contingents. People felt safer with the peacekeepers than with any of the warring factions. Experience had indeed taught Liberians a great and valuable lesson about trust, distrust and personal security—understandably so. Indeed, throughout the country, unarmed civilians—the ones for whom every faction claimed to have been fighting to liberate—remained ceaseless victims of heinous atrocities, at the hands of warring faction "liberators." Notable among these atrocities was the massacre in the St. Peter's Lutheran Church in Sinkor, Monrovia. That massacre occurred in July 1990 during the early days of the crisis. It is said to have been one of the most brutal of crimes against humanity, when soldiers of the Armed Forces of Liberia (AFL) entered the church and murdered 600 innocent civilians, including women and children, who fled their homes and sought refuge in the church. Over 150 more were wounded. Most of the victims were of the Gio and Minor tribes.

I can still recall vividly the night of the massacre. I had just left my church—the S. Trowen Nagbe United Methodist Church which is situated almost directly opposite the Lutheran Church. My church, like many churches at the time, was housing internally displaced people. As a church staff person on the relief committee, I had slept two nights at the church, sorting out food and other items for distribution to the people. This night, I had retired to spend some time with my family, just four blocks from the Methodist Church. During the shooting that lasted most of the night and into the early morning, we thought the rebels had entered the city and were exchanging fire with the government soldiers. It was not until the next morning that we learned otherwise.

I was among the first group of people to visit the scene of the massacre. Bodies littered the yard, the main streets and alleys. There was a baby on the back of his mother; he was still alive and crying, but the mother was dead. We were forbidden by solders from getting the baby or to even enter the church yard. The child was later taken by a woman in the community to care for him as her own. The bodies in the churchyard and in the streets around the church were buried, but the hundreds within the church remained unburied for many months.

Today, there are two mass graves in the church compound. Many believed that this grotesque violence by the AFL was ostensibly meant as reprisal against the people of Nimba County who comprised a larger percentage of the rebel faction of the NPFL at the time, and from whose region the war was begun. Others believed it was meant to discourage recruitment to the National Patriotic Front of Liberia (NPFL).

Another massacre of equal magnitude and heinousness occurred on June 6, 1993. The NPFL, it was believed, hacked several hundred men, women and children to death. That massacre became known as the Carter Camp Massacre. Carter Camp is a settlement on the Firestone Rubber Plantation. Initially, it had been rumored that the Armed Forces of Liberia, under the command of the then Commander-in-Chief Dr. Amos C. Sawyer, president of the Interim Government of National Unity, was the culprit for the Carter Camp atrocities because goods looted from the dead were found dumped around AFL positions in the Firestone area[5]. Later, through unsolicited confessions of many NPFL fighters, the genuine truth emerged.

Truth may be hindered, but as sure as the sun that rises in the east, it will come out bright and hot. Although a United Nations investigation team concluded in a report that the AFL committed the act and the team cited substantial evidence supporting its findings, the Interim Government and the AFL disputed the U.N. team's report, insisting on NPFL culpability. Survivors of the massacre named some key and well known AFL soldiers who, it was said, led their men to carry out this gruesome act. There are claims that the massacre was arranged by the NPFL in order to discredit the efforts of ECOMOG. The victims were buried in mass graves on the outskirts of the camp.

The Cow Field Massacre on Duport Road, a suburb of Paynesville, was another act of violence against innocent civilians. Another reason why people feared being in an area with any fighting group. About 48 people (all civilians) were massacred and burnt whilst they were asleep at their homes at Cow Field[6]. The perpetrators of this massacre remained unidentified, although survivors and residents of the area have pointed fingers at Taylor's NPFL. The victims were buried in the Palm Grove Cemetery on Center Street, in central Monrovia. The massacre was reported by the *News Newspaper* on December 19, 1994. Nearly every region of the country had its share of atrocities—from Grand Kru to Grand Bassa, from Nimba to Lofa, from Sinoe to Bomi and Cape Mount! No wonder why people preferred to be within the area of the African regional peace keepers than in a community with any warring faction.

So, for my family and Cedrick's, the plan was set: Freeport was the destination and leaving the country, our ultimate goal. By now, on this April day of 1996, it was dusk, and walking the streets after daylight was risky for anyone who was not an armed personnel. We were not willing to take this risk; not with our families.

Darkness was quietly settling upon us while we were yet a long way from the port. Our hearts sank as we realized that we would still be outside of the Freeport gate after sundown. Of course, it would be suicidal to walk the streets after dark. There were no street lights. But, as always, we remembered that the Lord provided our needs; and what we needed was a place to spend the night. We had now reached the area where Nora's sister lived. Although Nora had neither seen nor heard from her in a while, we decided to give it a try and go to the house. One of two things was certain to happen: 1) if Nora's sister was home, that would be wonderful; (2) if Nora's sister was absent, some family member or someone would be there who knew Nora as the sister, and would let us in. This is one of the best things that came out of the war; relatives and friends were always welcoming of others, willing to host them for a night or two or for however long they could. Most people, particularly, civilians, wanted to be helpful because none could ever tell when things would turn around and reciprocal help could be sought—a clear evidence of the old saying, "one good turn deserves another." Every act of kindness was a seed sown to be reaped in time to come. In some instances, though, precaution was taken not to let the wrong people into the home and fall into a serious problem. By wrong people, it could be members of an opposing faction fleeing and unsuspectingly coming to seek rescue. If such people were taken in and identified by another faction in the area, the receiving family could be entirely wiped out. It was therefore important that people knew whom they allowed into their homes.

We walked across the street on a single walking pathway to Nora's sister's place. The house was located about a quarter of a mile from the main street, in an area called Topo Village, which is a low land area usually flooded during the raining season. There were large puddles of water everywhere. Some neighbors peeped at us through their windows and doors to see who the new comers into their community were. This curiosity at the time was rooted in two factors. First: the fear that the new comers could be fighters of other factions, infiltrating on reconnaissance into the area and posing as civilians, only to bring in their forces to later carry out atrocities. These kinds of suspects were called "co-nnapers"—a local corruption of "connivers"—people conniving with rival factions. Second: the new comers could be people pursued by another armed group, thereby posing danger to the lives of other people living in the area. In a situation like that, it would be difficult to identify the ones being pursued from the people already living in the community; and anyone could become a culprit and be victimized. Such misadventures had happened before, and it was common in many communities. Strangers moved into an area; they were welcomed by residents, only to realize they were fighters awaiting signals to turn on the very people who had welcomed them. At other times, a fighting group would pursue a group of people and end up hurting other people within the communities to which the fleeing people had come. Such acts were perpetuated easily because it is difficult to differentiate one Liberian from another. We all basically look alike; there are no distinguishing marks that make one a 'fighter,' and the next even a 'pastor.' Any action against a group of people at any time invariably affected the good as well as the bad; in most instances, the innocent people suffered the most. Thus, the casualty of the civil war against civilians was so very high.

Whatever it was, the inquisitiveness of neighbors as we entered the community was understandable. We spoke politely as we passed by, and being friendly apparently eased their apprehension. In some spots, in the wet community, we had to walk on pieces of broken blocks to avoid stepping in the dirty water. We finally arrived at the house. Nora's sister, Theresa, was clearing some things from her porch and preparing to go inside. Interestingly, Theresa and I had been classmates in high school, but I did not know she was related to Nora. In fact, I knew both of them at two different times and never during these later years of knowing Nora, did I get to encounter Theresa. Nonetheless, we were both delighted to see each other. It was about 7:05pm and it had been 9 hours since we began the journey. The children were all exhausted, needing shower and bed. They were sweaty and sticky from the long walk in the burning sun. Theresa was more than welcoming to us. To our advantage, some earlier guests in her home had left for the Freeport a couple of days earlier, and so there were rooms to host our little group. We were 11 in all: 5 from the Reeves and 6 from my family. We were settled in two rooms for the night. Our wives jumped straight into preparing something to eat. At last, it was worth the journey; we had a place to lay our heads and rest. We were thankful to God for protecting us up to the moment, and to our host for providing a place. After showering and having something to eat, we prayed and went to bed.

"The Freeport of Monrovia was a safe haven
for many people. Thousands had fled into the port
area for safety and refuge. They were scattered all
over the port."

THE FREEPORT

The Freeport of Monrovia is the main commercial port facility in Liberia. It was constructed on Bushrod Island near Monrovia in 1948.

As early as 1850, ships began exporting palm oil from what might be called an irregular harbor, since regular harbors had not been constructed at Monrovia. Also, during World War II, the American military forces sought to export raw rubber from Liberia for wartime use. For that reason, the Americans improved the port facilities in Monrovia and built what was then a modern harbor breakwaters.In 1948, this new 750 acres (3.0 km2) bay opened. The national government took over the port from an American company in 1971 and created the National Port Authority to operate the facility. Today, it is referred to as "The Gateway to Liberia's Economy."[7]

The port facility consists of four piers and one main wharf with four berths; tanker facilities and a fishery pier. However, at the time of our trip in April 1996, due to the civil war which paralyzed government infrastructures, the port was operating at less than half capacity, and was under the control of the West African Peace Keeping Force, ECOMOG, who used it as one of their major bases—primarily for access to the seaway for bringing in their military hardware, personnel, food and other logistics. Operation of the port by ECOMOG was essential to its peace-keeping mission because entry into the country by air was almost nonexistent. Also, there was no other usable seaport.

The next morning, the entrance to the Freeport was packed with many persons seeking to enter. A long line extended up to a quarter of a mile from the front of the gate to the side of the main street. It was manned by ECOMOG soldiers who were searching individuals before they entered the port area. This process was necessary to ensure that no armed men slipped into the port to cause havoc. We joined the line and waited our turn. Hours passed before we reached the checking area. Our luggage, food and bodies were searched and cleared. We entered the port. Thousands of people had fled into the port area for safety and refuge. They were scattered all over the port. Almost every empty container was an apartment for a family or group of people.

On the pier was a small fishing boat called *Bulk Challenge*. Rumors had it that the charterer of the boat and the captain were planning to evacuate people to Ghana and/or Nigeria. It was a Nigerian vessel. In the early days of the war, in 1990, a Nigerian vessel – Zolotesa – evacuated thousands of Liberians to Nigeria and Ghana. So, we made inquiries and learned that the *Bulk Challenge* vessel was sailing to Nigeria but would first make a passenger drop stop in Ghana.

By the end of the day, nothing promising about our travel arrangement had been achieved. Nevertheless, we were not disappointed. At least we were in the port and were much safer. But then, there was nowhere to sleep. People were everywhere – in containers, offices and even in the open. Because we had many little children, we went back to Theresa's house and retired for the day. The house was not far from the port, and the community seemed calm and not troubled by what was going on in the port. Perhaps, this apparent sense of security was because of the community's proximity to the port and the security that the presence of the ECOMOG brought to the area.

The next day we went back to the port and repeated the check-in process. This time, it was just Cedrick and I. The rest of the family – women and children – remained home with strict instructions about what to do, just in case they observed strange movements or heard anything fishy. At the port, there was still uncertainty as to what would happen; there was no clear understanding about the ship or its departure. We began to meet several people we knew; they had now made the port their new home. These were people from our community up town, people from school, work and church. Even some distant family members were among them. I ran into some of my cousins who informed me that they had spoken to their brother who had promised to help them get out of the country if and when it was clear what the ship would do. We agreed to keep each other posted on news regarding the ship, departure and cost when the information became available. They took us to their spot, the area at the port where they now spent their days and nights. We continued to hang around an office within the port that was said to be used by the crew from *Bulk Challenge*. It was not a big enough ship for the crowd. If anything, it would have to be a first-come, first-serve basis, but under no circumstance could it take every one who wanted to get out. And then, we soon realized that not everyone at the port was there to get out. Some people just wanted to be in the safety reach of the peace keepers until things quieted down and they could go back to their homes, while others were there scouting for food and any other assistance they could get for their family.

One important function the Freeport served during the war years was, as market ground for food and other basic necessities. People assembled at the port each day to find food for their families. There was no telling what one might find on any given day. The goods on the market depended on contents of whatever warehouse was broken into. Sometimes there was food, which everyone needed; and sometimes such things as plates and glasses or paint, which nobody wanted. "Such was the time, such was the situation"—to quote Frank E. Tolbert, the brother of the late president, William R. Tolbert, Jr. Sadly, both had perished in the April 1980 military coup in the country. People came from nearby communities like Logan Town, New Kru Town, Clara Town and Battery Factory, to hustle for food for their families. People also came from far off places like Coca Cola Factory, Brewersville, and Central Monrovia. They left at the end of each day with whatever they could lay their hands on. Hence, it was understandable that not all the people in the port were there to leave the country. For us who had decided to leave, it was important that we kept our ears open for news of departure in order to be among the first to jump aboard. After a couple of days, we learned that the crew was considering a process to register potential passengers. I therefore managed to start a discussion and build relationship with some of the crew members. We had money to use to pay our way out of the country but did not know what it would cost for all of us. Once the word was out about the ship's plans, my cousin – the Rev. Dr. Larry Konmla Bropleh – connected with me to include his siblings in whatever plan or arrangement I was making. Larry was the Director for African Affairs of the Baltimore-Washington Conference of the United Methodist Church. He had visited Liberia twice in 1994 and 1995, and was in regular contact with relatives and friends. We connected Larry to the shipping authorities so that he would negotiate with them on our behalf. It took a couple of days for arrangements to be finalized because it was difficult to reach Liberia by phone at the time. However, payment arrangement was discussed and concluded, and Larry instructed us to go and meet the captain pay the money we had, and he would pay the difference. The cost was $75 per person. We went and met the captain, and he confirmed the agreement, and we paid for our tickets. The Captain listed our names and gave tickets for all 14 of us, including my family of six.

We were among the first group of people to be issued tickets. So, we were indeed excited that at long last, we would finally be leaving the hostilities behind. The instruction was simple: when it was time to board, heads of households or families would be called first to stand at the entrance while members of the family would be called; in our case, the 13 others. As they entered the ship, with tickets in hand, the head of the family or group would confirm that each belonged to that group. And they would all enter. It sounded really simple but didn't look so simple. Many people expressed fear that the growing number of people gathering to board the ship clearly exceeded the capacity of the ship. But the captain assured us repeatedly that we would be among the first to board.

There was sufficient funds — at least, enough money for the upkeep of my family for a couple of months. At the time, I worked as an Internal Auditor for the Liberia Bank for Development and Investment (LBDI). Thanks to the management who had arranged for its staff to get extra emergency money and food. By word-of-mouth, the message got around fast and we converged at the home office of a businessman at a certain location across the bridge. "Across the bridge"— the Freeport is situated on Bushrod Island, which is connected to central Monrovia by two bridges—the Waterside Bridge, referred to as the old bridge, and the Gabriel Tucker Bridge, referred to as the new bridge. Any location after the bridges is generally referred to as 'across-the-bridge.' At the home office, the General Manager and Comptroller paid staff and provided each of us a bag of rice. I got my pay and rice and was quite ready to get out of the country with some level of satisfaction. Although we had learned from experience how to hide money on ourselves, it was not reasonable to walk around with a whole lot of money, so I divided what I had received into two equal amounts and gave one half to my wife to hold and I held on to the other half.

The Liberia Bank for Development and Investment was one of the few surviving banks in the country and very much potent financially. Since its creation by an Act of the National Legislature in 1961, it has been one of the financial pillars of the country, perhaps because of its joint ownership by the Liberian government and major international financial institutions that purchased equity in the Bank. It is predominantly a privately owned institution under private management with a Board of Directors elected annually by its shareholders. The Bank commenced operations in 1965 as Liberian Bank for Industrial Development and Investment. Under an amendment in 1974, the name was changed to the Liberian Bank for Development and Investment (LBDI). A further amendment in 1988 allowed the Bank to engage in commercial banking activities, to complement its development objectives[8]. I was with the bank from 1993 to 1998.

With tickets in hand, and the assurances of the captain, we felt relaxed and satisfied that we would soon leave the horrors of the senseless war behind. To ensure we followed the development of the *Bulk Challenge* in regard to departure or any arrangement for leaving, we moved from Rebecca's house to the port and secured an empty 40-foot container as our new home. When my wife suggested it, at first I was edgy about staying in a container, because I thought I could find one of the offices on the compound, but they were all filled. Later, I realized that we were not the only family staying in a container. Many others had been there – in the Port – since they moved from their homes a while before the resurgence of fighting that April. All through the day and sometimes in the night, we strolled around the dock waiting to hear news of the departure of the ship, but we heard nothing. Each day was embraced with optimism but ended with frustration and uncertainty. Days went by and the crew kept issuing tickets and accepting money from potential passengers.

Finally, the day arrived and an officer announced on a loud speaker that luggage would be loaded onto the ship. He directed those with tickets to move their luggage nearer to the pier, and emphasized that ticket holders needed to be available to verify their luggage and take receipt of individual recovery tickets which they would need for claiming their luggage when the ship arrived at the planned destination. We rearranged our belongings, including personal credentials such as diploma, degrees, and certificates, and other important personal and family documents. We got on line like all other passengers with their belongings. There were so many look-alike luggage items that it was easy to get things mixed up. Therefore, we put special markings to identify ours. In addition, we had to constantly keep watch on our luggage so that no one would steal them or remove things from within them. In this crowd, as would always be the case, there were people of all sorts: the good, the bad and the ugly. Some were there because they desperately wanted to travel; some were there just for the safety of the port; and there were those—the hustlers—who were there to take advantage of others. Such people can be found in every situation and under every circumstance. So we were watchful and monitored our only belongings. I say "only" because this was all we had. Whatever was left at home would be gone by the time we returned. It would be taken by the rebels, or by people in the community. That was the trend.

When people left their homes for fear of their lives, the rebels who entered the community would loot the abandoned homes. If the rebels didn't do the looting, it would be returning neighbors who looted and then sold the looted things for little or nothing, just to get some money to buy food. When it came to hunger, most people just became mean to one another. I am reminded of the time we returned home in early 1990. The house was a total mess. Everything we left when we moved out was taken away by unknown individuals. Whatever few worthless items left behind were strewed all over the place. We had to start from scratch. The only household item we purchased was a sponge mattress that we put on the floor and slept on. No one wanted to buy expensive household items, since it was likely that running from place to place was imminent.

In those early 1990 days, when we had returned home, one day, I was strolling by the Antoinette Tubman Stadium (ATS). Soon, I spotted a book that looked like a book I used in graduate school. I didn't want to believe it because where we lived on 9th Street was approximately many miles from the ATS. But as I walked closer and looked harder, I discovered that indeed it was my book. I opened it and I saw my name and personal stamp; "I. Ezax Smith Family Library." Curiosity led me to open a few other books and certainly, the guy was selling my entire bookshelf. "Ain't this something?" I thought to myself, considering the distance from my house to where this guy had his sidewalk book stand. I informed the vendor that the books he had were mine and showed him my ID. All he said was, *"if you need any of these books, you will have to buy them. I am doing business, and I don't know you."* Then he went on to tell the price I would have to pay if I needed any. I could not believe my ears. But I knew better than to argue or fuss over books that had practically no value at the time, to me. Moreover, I also knew what the consequence of trying to talk about getting them back could be. For one, I did not have money. Secondly, the stadium is across from the Barclay Training Center, a military barracks. That meant that this vendor could be an army personnel, a soldier or relative of a soldier. Any argument would be severely detrimental to me. I could get arrested, beaten or worst, killed. Finally, I concluded I really did not have need for any book. What would I be doing with books during this war time when I could possibly be running again? What would I be doing with books when I needed food for my children? I politely walked away thinking to myself how many persons like me could be finding their precious belongings with other people in the streets of Monrovia. Ironically, this sort of activity (selling stolen things) got so rampant that many areas around the city became known as the *"Buy-Your-Own-Thing Market"* - like a thrift yard sale.

A notable "Buy-Your-Own-Thing Market" of this sort was located on Johnson Street. Others were in places like Paynesville Red Light and Duala Market. At these sites, one could buy anything for cheap. This was where most people went to restart their lives and get basic things like pots, pans, spoons, cups, chairs and mattresses or bed sheets. Anything could be found here including one's own things, but they had to be paid for, with no questions asked as to how the items got to the market. It was an interesting experience, but this too was the war and the effects of the war.

"After many days of waiting, the fear of
uncertainty was reduced as the crew began
loading luggage into the ship."

LUGGAGE ON BOARD

The day arrived and the crew began loading luggage into the hatch or hull of the vessel. Like the belly of a whale, the hatch of the ship could surely hold a lot of things. It took in cars, motorcycles, computers, beds, TVs, radios, tables, desks, couches, window frames, and pipes. It swallowed up the scraps taken from the tracks of the railroads, used tires and old car frames; mattresses, washing machines and refrigerators. For three full days the soldiers and crew loaded things belonging to them; things they had either purchased on the black market or taken as war-loot. Too many things were being loaded that I was beginning to wonder how much luggage of the traveling population, scattered all over the port yard, would get on the ship. But my skepticism became less and less only as the crew began to load luggage after luggage into the ship. Two times during the loading process I checked with the captain to ensure our portion of the long list was not tugged to the bottom of the pile from which he was calling. After all, it had been days of loading and our names were yet to be called. We watched suitcases, bags, barrels, bundles, and all sorts of paraphernalia get loaded on board. It was a tiresome process with everyone pushing through the crowd to the center area to keep eyes on personal items and listen to their names. The process went like this: your name would be called from the master registration list; when you responded, the crew verified that you were the person by the show of some form of identity (passport, work ID or the National ID); your luggage items were then identified and placed in the net of the crane or lifter, and loaded into the hatch of the ship.

It was amazing to learn how much architectural and engineering skills are put into shipbuilding—the design and construction, leading to the unprecedented size and complexity. Ultimately, a ship looks somewhat small from the outside but extremely huge on the inside.

With every additional luggage loaded, I marveled at the holding capacity of that little ship. Hour after hour, and luggage after luggage, the ship swallowed up tons and tons of personal and household items. The yard was clearing but there was much more to get on board. While the loading was in progress, we noticed people getting on board as well. Whether it was official, we could not tell but they kept getting on board.

After a couple of days of loading, I heard my name called over the loud speaker. I was a little distance away from the center area. So, I pressed my way through the crowd, repeatedly saying, "Excuse me, it's my name; excuse me, they just called me." I could see the excitement on the faces of my family as they learned that our things would be finally loaded on board the ship. I reached the officer on the podium and showed him my ID, and then I pointed to our luggage. It was tagged onto the lifter and loaded into the hatch. With a sigh of relief, I went to my container-home and had a restful night for the first time in days, thankful I did not have to spend one more night keeping watch over the things.

After two days, the crew began calling names for people to board the ship. I listened with eager expectation of getting on board soon enough to secure a suitable space on the ship. The number of people on board kept growing. All the while, I still did not hear my name called. A disappointing feeling came upon me as I observed how the crew coordinated the boarding process. They seemed not to be following the list in a sequential order. It should have been on a first-come-first-serve basis but some crewmen and soldiers kept taking money on the side from people who did not officially register or purchase tickets and putting them on board. Although the registration process was closed, these crewmen were receiving as low as $25 and $20 from individuals to get them on board, outside of the official process. *What a corrupt process*! I thought. For a while, the concentration was on the area beside the ship where men, women and children were illegitimately being thrown overboard into the ship. Legitimate ticket holders were becoming impatient as the number of illegal boarders continued to increase. "If this continues, there will be no space for the legitimate ticket holders," I mentioned to some of the individuals with tickets in their hand. Imagine, we had paid $75 per person and we kept on line waiting to be called, but that was not happening.

THE SUDDEN TAKE-OFF

It happened very fast and so unscrupulously that neither the passengers on board nor the multitude on the dock knew what was happening. It had been a while since the authorities of the ship called any names to get on board. There were hundreds of families waiting to be called, mine included, who had tickets in hands and luggage already on board the ship. All the while, soldiers on the side of the ship were collecting money from individuals and putting them on the ship.

For some of us, that practice would not go unspoken about, particularly since the ship was just about overcrowded. "Well," I said to my family, "I am going on board to meet with the captain, and if it is not possible to get us on, they'll need to reimburse our money." As for the things already on the ship, we would make arrangement with an acquaintance on the ship to take delivery of them in Ghana. It was not the best thought but a probable initial alternative in the event that we were reimbursed because we could not travel with the ship. I made my way to the side of the ship where all the corruption was taking place. As I approached the stairs, a soldier stopped me and asked for what I had to pay. I showed him my ticket and told him I was going on board to speak with the captain regarding my family's situation. He said no. I insisted that I had a right to see the captain since I had paid for my space on the ship. The second soldier joined us by this time and, without asking, began whipping me with a rubber cord. He wanted me to get off the stairs so that people with money could get on. I reiterated my claim that I had already paid and wanted to see the captain.

By this time, some others in the same situation as I was,

gathered at the bottom of the stairs and shouted support for me. In the heat of the commotion, a senior officer standing on board called out to the officers to allow me to speak with him. I went up and politely explained my situation and pleaded to speak with the captain. Evidently, this officer had seen me earlier in discussion with the captain and said, "Okay, no problem. I'll let you see him." He directed me to the cabin and I made my way to the captain's cabin. It was a tough time going through. The ship was full to capacity, and walking among the passengers, I knew there was no way we could get on that vessel. It looked scary: people sitting everywhere. As I got into the cabin area, I saw a large crowd already in the hallway complaining about the unjust treatment. Many people in the crowd were demanding their money and also their luggage items from the hatch. Of course this was an unreasonable request, because it would mean for all of the people already on board to get off prior to opening the hatch to retrieve luggage. Nevertheless, I could understand the anger, especially, of those who had bought their tickets but seemingly had no space on the ship. I tried pressing my way through the crowd to the captain but met with resistance from the people before me.

I felt hot sweat roll down my back; my shirt was sticking to my body. The mix of body odor, cologne and perfume, food and machine oil produced an unpleasant scent. I almost vomited when a guy lifted his arm to signal someone from across the aisle. A whiff of air shot out stench similar to that of an old wet dirty foot of socks stuck in an old shoe for very long time. The odor of that guy's armpit tore through my nostrils.

The price for heading a group can be more than what can be easily imagined. The responsibilities of leadership can be a difficult experience. You become the sacrifice for the people you lead. Such was the situation; we had to take it all in: the good with the bad; the fighting, and talking, and sometimes unbearable beatings, to justify the leadership role. I continued to push my way through, never for a moment considering the time spent in that cabin hallway. Just before I could reach the cabin door, the captain came out and called the mob to attention. He explained in calm, reassuring voice that all the people with tickets were going to be called on board. He further noted that he was investigating some officers who had put people on the ship without authorization. According to him, the ship was going to be swept to eject anyone on board who could not show a registration ticket. He apologized to the group and promised to do all in his power to ensure that all ticket-holders got on board.

With that said, all of us – angry ticket-holders – turned back to take the news of comfort to our inpatient families. I was a little doubtful, but decided to take him by his word. While we were confident we had made head ways with arguing our case, the captain and crew had, to our dismay, planned to take off once they got rid of us and we were on the ground. They calculated that once we got off the ship, it would be difficult to get back onto the ship. Apparently, they reasoned this was their best strategy in light of how vicious Liberians had become since the onset of the civil war. Destruction of property had become second nature, and people would feel no remorse tearing down this ship with crooked crewmen who tried to rob them of the opportunity to get out of the danger.

Come to think about it, the captain's polished and apologetic statement was not sincere at all. There was no way, after the struggle to get on, anyone on that ship would have disembarked so easily and lose their space. No way. The captain had simply lied to us, period. The ship crew was not trying to check for ticket-holding passengers; they were not going to request anyone to get off the ship; they were not planning to bring the hundreds in the dockyard on board either. They had created a messy situation that they could not repair. Thus, in order to avoid possible catastrophe that could result if the group in the dockyard decided to revolt, they took off discretely and unceremoniously. It was a dirty plan, a trick with complete disregard to people who had paid their hard-earned money.

When I got through the crowd and onto the deck, I noticed that the ship had already withdrawn anchor from the pier; it was gradually drifting into the ocean. The pace between the ship and the dock was not narrow enough to take a leap; and for fear of the risk of injuring myself, I did not. I was 32 years old then; and even though I still had it in me to do some artistic acrobatic high jump, I decided not to. I looked down and there was my wife, standing with some food and water in a bag—at least enough to last the three or four days estimated journey to Ghana. She threw the bag overboard and I assured her that I would recover our things and make my way back to them as soon as possible. She understood it was not an intentional decision to leave just like that, but one of necessity. She cautioned me to be careful and to take care of myself. I admonished her to take care of the children and herself. We were shouting over all the noises and turmoil. At least I was satisfied she could manage the kids with what she had for the next couple of weeks until I returned. I also had some money to serve my going, staying and returning.

Later on the journey, I discovered that 90% of the people who were in the cabin's hallway with me also did not make it back on land to their people. We were all caught up in the trap of the crewmen. We were all tricked into leaving by force and against our will. Was this fate or mere coincidence? I could not comprehend the rapidity with which things had all unfolded. More anger set in and I was tempted, as were the others, to go back to the captain to inquire why he had lied to us; why he had taken our money under false promise; and why the ship was leaving without words to the hundreds of people to whom they were obligated, but I couldn't. I could hardly move from where I was. Every inch of space around me was occupied by someone. Moreover, the crew had closed the door to the cabin area. So, if we could get through the crowd we would not be able to make it to the captain. I just stood in the spot where I was and looked at the port area as it gradually faded away.

Speechless for a while, I just stood and looked with teary eyes as the entire city disappeared before me. The ship slashed through the waves; the dark water parted to give way to this huge moving machine. The water still looked dark and dirty as we made our way into farther distance of the ocean. I felt deceived, anger overtook me, and I wanted to do something awful to the people who owned the ship - knowing that a bigger part of me – my family – was left behind. I looked again into the water and then I saw my shadow and those of many others looking back at me. The atmosphere felt like our spirits were guiding the journey. It brought a sudden sense of confidence to look, with hopefulness, to the days ahead. About 30 minutes into the journey, the boat came to a standstill; it was not moving at all and nobody knew why. People started speculating as to why we were not moving. After another 25 minutes, we saw a tug boat come by with Tom Yoweyou, Alhaji Kromah and a few other prominent individuals who were either participants in the war or in the leadership of a warring faction. They got on, and the boat continued the journey. I was not too satisfied or happy with this move but there was nothing I or anyone could do about it. They had sought protection with the peacekeepers out of fear for their own safety and were escaping just as we were. After hours of standing, I finally sat on the stairs leading to the upper deck of the ship. There was only one space left on those stairs; and rightly so, because that was where I was standing the whole while. If I had left for any reason, I would not have had that spot. I sat and it became my room for the rest of the journey.

I had traveled by ship once, in 1992, en route to Budapest, Hungary for the 41st International Congress of AIESEC, the largest student run organization in the world, which provides students with leadership training and internship opportunities in for-profit and non-profit organizations. AIESEC[10] is the French acronym for *Association internationale des étudiants en sciences économiques et commerciales* (English: International Association of Students in Economic and Commercial Sciences). I was one of the

representatives of the national chapter of Liberia when we made
the trip. Although there was cessation of hostilities in the country at
the time, the insecurity made it difficult for flights to come into or
fly out of the country. As a result, the only way out of the country
was by the ECOMOG helicopter or ship to a neighboring country,
from where travel arrangements would be made. Attempts to fly
out in the helicopter did not materialize so we went with the
ECOMOG ship from Monrovia to Accra before flying off to
Hungary. The experience was different. There was more rooms
and we were in the ship cabins rather than on the deck. I remember
seeing the city disappear but not as slowly as it was the night we
made the sudden departure on May 5th 1996. Moreover, there was
nothing particular to look at that time – all visibility on land had
vanished; only the wide open ocean and blue sky were in sight. The
ship traveled into deep sea. But this night was different in countless
ways: we continued to see features from on land as long as we
traveled – houses, trees, towers, etc. And then again, I seemed
empty. It was as if something had left my body and spirit. I couldn't
quite put my hand on what it was or what was wrong; just a feeling
of emptiness. But one thing was for sure—I had family back there:
my wife and children; all I had ever worked for; all I could claim as
my own were left standing on the dock. I could imagine the
thoughts running through my children's little minds: "Will Daddy
come back?" "What if something happened to us, how will Daddy
know?" "Will the food last Daddy the duration of the ship? "What
if, what if, what if…."

Not only was I imagining what my children were thinking; I
myself began to question the whole journey and situation. Many
thoughts ran through my mind as well. Of course, it had to. I was
leaving my wife and children not just behind, but in a combat
environment that could be very explosive and highly dangerous.
Who would they turn to if things got much worse? How would
they get around easily without my male presence? What if
something happened to my family? What if they were attacked?

What if someone attempted to take advantage of them? What if they ran out of money or food?

Those thoughts can be frightening, but instead of being scared, I allowed the thoughts of my family to be my source of strength. If I had to survive the journey to and from wherever we landed, it had to be because of them – my family. They were the purpose for which I live. We had all been fighting for nearly six years; fighting in many different capacities - fighting to survive; fighting hunger; fighting diseases; fighting fear; and fighting the uncertainties of the war. But here I was, leaving the country, not with my family, as I had planned, but by circumstances beyond my control, without the little ones and without my dear wife. I wished I could reverse what was occurring, for my mind was fighting the reality of being aboard this ship and moving further and further away from home.

But how could I stop it? One might argue that I could have jumped overboard if I wanted to, but from the position I was at the time, it was highly unlikely, unsafe and dangerous. Fate must have its way. I thought about all the pleasant and unfortunate things that could possibly occur and reasoned against the odds that it would be well. Sometimes, you have to listen to that still small voice that speaks from within you; particularly, when you have prayed under the circumstances I faced at the moment. There is little you can do and when you have no control over what can and cannot be, it's time you give it up. As I have grown older and stronger in my faith as a Christian, I've come to develop a personal philosophy of life with deep spiritual connotation. And that is, "when things don't seem to go the way I expect— especially after exploring all options—and when it seems I have no control over the situation, circumstance, or event, I resign myself to the Lord. I say, "Lord, I don't know what this is and why it is the way it is; I don't seem to understand nor see my way through it; so, I turn it over to you. Whatever you have in it for me, let your will be done." Time after time, the situation has worked out to my advantage. The great lesson I've learned over the years is that sometimes the obstacles we face are only intended to create a delay and to prepare us so God can work out His purpose in our lives. We do not need to push everything to the limits; just let it be and wait, as scripture says, "...and see the salvation of the Lord."

The scripture, Romans 8:28 (NIV) becomes evident each time under these circumstances, "...for we know that all things work together for good, to them that love the Lord and are called according to His purpose." Because I am a believer, this verse comes alive and is relevant in numerous situations I just don't seem to understand, and conditions that my best efforts cannot change. We are often tempted to limit God to certain situations and think that others are too big for God. But, like other have said, "We need to stop telling God how big our problems are, and start pointing our problems to the BIG God we serve." This is so true, for that is what Romans 8:28 means – ALL things – not some things; not certain things; not occasional things; but ALL things. The promise in this is "God will work it out for your good." It is not our place to size up what things we commit to God; it is not up to us to determine which things are appropriate or not for God. All we have to do is turn it all over to him, and let God be God in every situation.

Sometimes the situation may be pleasant and sometimes it may be unpleasant; sometimes good and sometimes bad. Sometimes these circumstances have outrageous beginnings and ugly encounters; from the onset, we think are the worst coming for us; but only in the end, to realize that they were the best things that could have happened. Whatever it is, let God use it to accomplish His purpose in your life.

So, as we slowly drifted from the pier and I had the opportunity to sit for the first time after three hours of standing, I bowed my head and said a prayer. I talked to God in a personal way. Then I heard the Lord say, "It will be alright." I have a strong-willed, hard-working, dedicated, committed and independent wife but I needed the assurance from God. And when I felt in my spirit that I had received it, I resigned all my fears and concerns and looked forward to the presumed three-day journey to Ghana.

A HORRIFIC SAIL

Several days have passed since the ship took off from the Freeport of Monrovia. Each day went by so slowly that it seemed longer than a usual day; it was as if the day had 38 hours instead of 24. It had far exceeded the anticipated duration of the journey. What a slow ship!

The ship was built as a fishing vessel not intended for regular passenger travel. However, under the circumstance as ours – a forced evacuation – it could manage a capacity of up to 1500 people maximum. The number of people on this ship was well over 3700. Some estimated it was 4000 people. Could it safely carry the weight of the people and the extra tons of load in the hatch? After hours of sailing, one apparent observation was evident: we were still sailing in shallow waters along the coast of Liberia. We had not sailed into deep waters. "Maybe for a few more hours we will," I thought to myself. I remembered when I first traveled by ship we went away from the coastlines and deep into the ocean, and all we saw at the time was the wide ocean - water on all sides of the ship. Nothing else was in sight. However, here on this trip, we were nearly seven hours into the journey and were still seeing the trees and houses along the shores. No explanation for this was readily available until some time later. Night came and the area in which we were now sailing, was lot more refreshing as the sun had bowed its head to the cooling effect of the air coming from the belly of the ocean. The air had a kind of dampness about it but it was still invigorating compared to the blazing 80 degrees heat we had endured since morning. The water stretched as far as one could see. It's color changed from green to blue to grey, with the light of the sun by day. But now at twilight, you couldn't tell the ocean from the sky.

Ripples and waves continuously flowed, eventually breaking into foam at the end of the shoreline. The ocean made sounds like water surging and retreating against the ship. There was a smell of saltwater in the air, a scent like no other. "It won't be long," I thought. Two more days of sitting in the heat, and that would be it for the journey. Then morning came and to my utmost surprise, the ship had not yet covered the coast line of Liberia. We were somewhere between Sinoe and Maryland counties, in eastern Liberia. "Why is the sailing so slow? Why are we still close to the mainland? Is there something we should know that has not been told?" Curiosity was growing among passengers. we needed some answers as well as assurance that the ship was worthy of the journey. Somewhere between our thoughts and concerns was the startling reality that caught all passengers by surprise: the boat was slowly sinking, such that one could nearly touch the water from the deck. By the end of that third day, the rumors had become not only widespread, but confirmed – that the boat was slow and traveling along the coast because it had a hole, and that water had entered and was entering the hatch, so that the weight was increasing and causing the ship to slowly sink. It was like traveling in a canoe. Indeed, this explained how low the ship had been traveling. But that news was not received gracefully. Great fear gripped us all; it was nearly chaotic.

Everywhere, people were murmuring about death and the fear of death. They complained and cried like the children of Israel complaining in the wilderness. Can you imagine what was now running through my own mind? Of course, my family! The thought that I would lose my children and my wife, and be buried in *the* depth of the ocean, with no grave and no way of tracing my remains was unbearable. I knew of many deaths and of many mass graves and of families that would never know the final resting place of their loved ones. But I was not prepared to be a part of such statistics. "It can't be this bad," I thought. "Something will have to be done, and fast too. I know the captain and crewmen will find a way out." At the same time, my food had nearly run out. We were just midway crossing Maryland — still in Liberian territorial waters — and all my food was nearly finished. I had to cut back on my daily portion, but that didn't help much. The last of my food was consumed the day after we discovered the ship was leaking. Like me, not many people on board knew they would be without food and water for days to come. The general thought had been that the ship would take three to four days to reach Ghana. Those who had legally paid for the trip and had had the opportunity of boarding, before the unfortunate situation of people bribing their way on board, had prepared or had taken with them food to last the duration of the trip.

Without any prompt, a concert of prayer had begun all over the ship. In every section, people were praying - trusting God to take the ship to safety; praying that nothing disastrous happened before we docked. But with three days gone by and we were still within the Liberian territorial waters, it was a question of how long it would take before we reached a safe place or before the ship sinks. We were still a far way off and the only possible hope for any form of assistance was to make a stop in neighboring Ivory Coast. But this would have to be the captain's call and the Ivorian government's permission for the ship to stop over. Information circulated that the crew had made contact with the authorities to dock at San Pedro. It was interesting how information got around so fast; we had a way of getting and sharing information. I can't explain how it happened but it was effective and most often, accurate. If this latest information was true, it would be a blessing. We were closer to San-Pédro, a port town in southwestern la Côte d'Ivoire (Ivory Coast) situated about 40 miles (65 km) southwest of Sassandra on the Gulf of Guinea. Historical notes on the Sassandra reveal that until the mid-1960s, San-Pédro was a tiny fishing village of fewer than 100 inhabitants, but, following the start of port construction there in 1968, this village rapidly grew into a major town. Upon completion of the port in 1970, San-Pédro became the nation's second largest port city in southwestern Ivory Coast and the capital of the Bas-Sassandra Region. The city is served by San Pédro Airport. Largely developed from the 1960s, fishing is an important industry in the town, while the town is known for its nightlife and its beaches. Exports consist mainly of wood products, which also constitute the town's largest industry11.

The news that we would be heading for San-Pedro was a welcome thought as we got close to entering Ivorian territorial waters. Hopes were rising and spirits were being uplifted at the news that the Ivorian government would allow us to enter and dock at their port, if for nothing else but to examine the condition of the ship. It was quite evident that the ship was in real danger. Sitting on the deck, one could stretch downward and touch the water. The ship was moving much slower than when it had taken off. We knew now, with the information of a hole in the hatch, that this ship would not make it past the Ivory Coast. It would sink. It was just a matter of time, with the entry of more water, and we would all be dead; at least, most of those who could not swim. I was already making contingency plans in case the ship sank. I would grab on to one of the empty five-gallon rubber containers that belonged to one of the passengers, and use it as aid if I had to swim my way to the shore. And, although I can swim, I could not tell the actual distance the ship was from the main land. So, just in case, taking hold of the five-gallon container would be my back-up plan to help me stay afloat. I had my eyes fixed on that container, waiting for any eventuality. No one had access to the captain's cabin to know the status of negotiations being made between the crew and the Ivorian government, so we waited eagerly for the BBC news to feed us with the development along these lines. Each hour of the day we would gather around any available transmitter radio to hear our fate, because by now, the impending fate of the *Bulk Challenge* had reached the outside world. According to the news, some humanitarian organizations were making pleas to the Ivorian government on behalf of the ship and its passengers. So, there was some certainty that we would make landing in San-Pédro.

The city of San-Pédro was clearly in view but the ship was not yet granted permission to dock. We sat on the edge of the city and waited. While we waited, my mind tortured me. Would the people of San-Pédro and Ivory Coast watch the ship sink slowly with over 3500 people on it? This thought was not pleasant at all. I wondered how people could be so cruel, considering reports that the ship was carrying thousands of children and elderly, without food and water. The day was almost over and we had not heard anything positive, nothing promising. The crew pleaded, on humanitarian grounds, for the ship to be allowed to dock in order to carry out some repair work that would enable the ship to continue its journey to Ghana and/or Nigeria. Repeatedly, the Ivorian authorities refused on grounds that there were too many armed combatants on board; - an information communicated by Charles Taylor in a BBC pronouncement that we were all rebels. The truth is, there were few individuals on the ship who were associated with warring factions, but the vast majority of the people were ordinary citizens - pregnant women, children and old people – some of whom had begun to get seasick. It was understandable, the stance the Ivorian Government was taking, considering the Sierra Leone experience—where it was believed that rebels had crossed over from Liberia into Sierra Leone and launched similar civil war. This was a situation no other country in the region wanted to be repeated, but the situation in which we found ourselves was completely different. Couple of hours later, around about 3:00pm, we heard a new kind of report coming from a Medicins Sans Frontieres speed boat, by way of the BBC News. It said that the ship was going to sink because the weight was increasing as a result of the influx of water. It reported that people were dying on the ship and that the international community should get involved in persuading the Ivorian government to allow the ship into their port. The report further stated that the ship had run out of food and water and it had no emergency medical treatment or supplies. This was good news for us, knowing that someone other than the crew was pleading on our behalf. The reporters identified themselves as medical personnel who had followed the ship, knowing what danger it was in – not particularly because of the hole in the hatch but because of the over crowdedness.

"We were finally allowed entry into the Port of San Pedro for repair work.

…..the port officials barricaded portion of the pier with 20 and 40 feet containers to block-in an area large enough to hold the over 3500 people on board.

This was a decision of the authorities to ensure control of the crowd….."

SAN-P'EDRO: A BREADTH OF RELIEF

Out to sea, a little distance away, was a small boat with a four-man crew: three men and a woman. They were waving and showing up their thumbs – "the thumbs up" – as if to say: "It's going to be fine." Inscribed on the sail was the familiar "Medicins Sans Frontieres" (MSF) emblem. We shouted back, "Thanks for the report. Thanks for the report!" And then, we held up our thumbs in return; a sense of gratitude filled our hearts.

Medicins Sans Frontieres, also known as "Doctors without Boarders," is a secular humanitarian-aid, non-governmental organization best known for its projects in war-torn regions and developing countries facing endemic diseases. Its headquarters are in Geneva, Switzerland. The organization, which is known in most of the world by its French acronym, MSF, was created in 1971 by a small group of French doctors and journalists in the aftermath of the Biafra secession. These doctors and journalists believed that all people have the right to medical care regardless of race, religion, creed or political affiliation, and that the needs of these people outweigh respect for national borders[12]. MSF has been operating in Liberia since the inception of the Liberian Civil War. MSF first entered Liberia in 1990 to help civilians and refugees affected by the Liberian Civil War. Constant fighting throughout the 1990s and the April 1996 outbreak of battles which prompted the mass evacuation, kept MSF volunteers actively providing nutrition, basic health care, and mass vaccinations, as well as speaking out against attacks on hospitals and feeding stations, especially in Monrovia.

They were quite acquainted with the civil war, and particularly with the circumstances under which the ship departed Liberia. This team had followed the ship because they believed was in danger, keeping watch and monitoring the activities of the ship, until it was publicly announced on radio waves that the Ivorian government was not allowing the ship into its port. It was then that this team spoke out on the BBC, attesting to the fact that the ship was indeed in danger and calling on the international community to appeal to, or mount pressure on the Ivorian government to accept the ship.

It was a good report, particularly, coming from a third party with no special interest in the ship or the passengers. This news renewed our hope that, at least, someone might hear and do something for the hungry, sick and dying people on the ship. It did have a positive impact. The very next day, we learned that the ship would be allowed to dock in San-Pédro, but only for the purpose of patching or repairing the leakage. It was a breadth of relief. Praises rang throughout the ship; there were loud cheers everywhere. "At least, we will have the opportunity to *stretch our legs* a little bit, and walk around and buy something to eat and or drink," so I thought.

But as the ship approached the pier, it was clear that the *Bulk Challenge*'s passengers would not be allowed anywhere else within the city of San-Pédro except the port. The government was taking precaution to ensure that no disruption or disturbance affected economic and social activities in their city as a consequence of the presence of people from the ship. Hence, the port officials barricaded a portion of the pier with 20 and 40 feet containers to block-in an area large enough to hold the over 3000 people on board. This was a decision of the authorities to ensure control of the crowd, particularly due to the negative Intelligence that fighters were on the ship. It was said that Charles Taylor had communicated with authorities in the Ivory Coast not to allow the passengers off the ship – citing "they are all rebels." The authorities stacked two levels of containers – 17 feet high – and made a U shape about half the size of a football field. The containers extended few feet over the edge of the pier, overlooking the water.

The people of the community were very compassionate and empathetic toward us. They had been following the news of the risks of starvation because of lack of food and water. They rushed toward the ship with bread and water and other food items but they were prevented from going into the ship with the items. They waited with the food for a while but the soldiers asked them to vacate the space before we disembark. So, they threw the food and water overboard to whoever would get them, and I believe, so that we could distribute and share with one another. Some people caught them and were glad to have something to eat. I was not fortunate to catch any of the bread but did eat a piece from a neighbor who shared what he had caught. People were looking out for others in those desperate moments. We were all one and in the same predicament together. I learned later, that some people were angry with the Ivoirians for throwing the bread, and they in turn, threw the bread back at the Ivoirians. I didn't think that was necessary, especially, since the people were not allowed to get on the ship to deliver the food. I thought this was a sign of ingratitude, because the throwing of the food was conditioned on the fact that the people were not allowed to take them on the ship for obvious reasons. They could have been mistaken for someone on the ship, or someone on the ship could pretend to be one who had taken food on the ship. Whatever the situation, they were just trying to be helpful and I thought the least we could have done was be appreciative. Moreover, they were asked to clear the space, to get out of the area. The entrance to the space was manned by security forces, and used by port authorities and designated crewmen who had to either come in or go out to procure materials needed to repair the ship. They called for the elderly and women with children to disembark first. They were taken out of the contained area. Where to? I don't know. After a while, one by one we made our way down to the concrete pavement. At least, we were safely on land and hopeful of a solution to the problem. As more and more people came off the ship the smaller and smaller the space became, and the more difficult it was to use the outhouse. Before long, we were crammed in the area that once seemed a large space. The air was steamy and mixed with the scent of fresh ocean water.

There was not much room to move about, but hey, just standing and taking few steps around was enough of a comfort from sitting in one place for hours, if not days. But beyond the comfort of walking around, some people needed to drink, some to eat, and others to use the bath room, but no one was permitted to leave the boxed-in area. We looked like slaves being held for auction or for dispatch to a new land.

Outside the containers, a great crowd of men, women, students, religious and civic organizations, and people from all walks of life gathered. They had come to see the people from the "forsaken ship." Some had come to bring aid and help in whatever way they could, but the soldiers and police guarding the entrance prevented them from entering the shielded area. What a double trouble! We could not go out, and people coming to help could not come in. They offered to go and purchase food and drinks for those who wanted them. There was some skepticism as to whether people would ever return with the items they were asked to get. The truth is, if anyone decided not to return, there was nothing anybody could do about it. The odds were against us in many ways: we did not know to whom we were giving our money; neither did we have a way to make any report from behind the barricade if someone decided to take off. It was a "do-or-die" situation and everyone took the chance, trusting that the individuals offering to help would be faithful to their words to help the hungry people. Much to my anticipation and to others' amazement, they returned with bread, water, juices and lot more. Indeed, they were honest, helpful people — what the preachers would refer to as "The Good Samaritans." Far more astonishing were the massive humanitarian efforts by religious and civic groups and ordinary people who, using their own funds, purchased tons of food and other essentials, including bread, water and first aid kits and brought them to share with us. Through the entrance of the enclosed area, we received the items. This time, I was able to get three pieces of the 12- inch long bread—we call "Fula bread" in Liberia. I ate one of the pieces, drank small water and kept the others for the rest of my journey. I wished I had more, but others had to eat as well. I also had three bottles of water to take with me. For many people who did not have money to buy anything, this was a God-send gesture; and we were all thankful. At least, everybody had something to eat and drink, and to take with them back on the ship.

Four poly johns (portable toilets) were set up in the far left corner of the area. At first, I thought those four were sufficient for the crowd, but as people began to line up to use the poly johns, I realized the "johns" were far inadequate for the population on the ground. But that was all we could get. Some of us men could not stand to wait for the lines, and therefore eased ourselves on the side of the containers – as quickly as we could. We even walked around the entire encampment to see if some exits could be found, but much thought was placed in this makeshift architectural work such that no one could go around or over the containers.

A team of divers and engineers was engaged to examine the extent of the damage to the ship. It was determined that, indeed, there was a hole somewhere beneath the ship through which water had entered into the hatch. The items placed in the ship were all soaked, increasing the weight of the ship. The repair work was carried out simultaneously by two work groups: one was involved with pumping out the water from within the hatch; while the other, to seal the hole beneath the ship. For nearly seven hours or more, the teams worked tirelessly — intermittently checking to see if the ship was sea-ready. After several checks and reassessments, it was declared that the repair had been successfully completed and the journey was to resume. We climbed back into the ship, ready for the next leg of our journey. The feeling of being on land was uplifting but brief, while the anticipation of continuation was saddening and dreadful. Not many persons wanted to climb back

on board that ship, but there was no option. We had to leave.
When everyone was back on board, the ship took off for the second
time since leaving Liberia.

SURVIVING WITHOUT FOOD & WATER

Soon after the repairs, we boarded the ship and took off again eastbound toward Ghana and Nigeria. By this time, it was still unclear where our final destination would be. It was rumored that the Ghanaian authorities had issued an order not to allow the ship into its harbor. Notwithstanding the rumor, the ship continued in the eastbound direction. Ghana was a likely destination for many reasons, but primarily because many people had relatives and friends living on the Buduburam Refugee Camp; and secondly, because of its closer proximity to Liberia, should a voyager decide to go back home. For most passengers on the *Bulk Challenge*, including myself, it was a preferred ending point. My mother-in-law had been on the camp since 1990 and had established herself there. So if I was to go to Ghana, I would have a place to stay and someone to help me find my way around.

Three days passed since leaving San-Pédro and we still had not reached Ghana. My three loaves of "Fula" bread were consumed in two and a half days. It was nearly one day and couple of hours that I had not had anything to eat. For some strange reason, I did not even know the day of the week or the date. I seemed to have lost count. I wondered how many more days would we have to travel before reaching Ghana. I hoped not long. I still had one bottle of water left. I was very stingy with the water. I drank very tiny bits at a time. I did not share it with anyone. My bread was finished early because I was generous within my section of the ship. I shared with some of the people who did not have food, but my water, I kept it for myself. It was my life.

Across the deck of the ship I watched mothers and fathers, big
sisters and brothers, grandmothers and grandfathers starve
themselves for the sake of their children. What a sacrifice! All the
bread and other food they had received were saved for their
children and it was understandable. The young ones were most
vulnerable. They could not go long without food; so, those parents
with children took the pains of staying without food so that their
children would have it to eat. A number of times, I had to give up
pieces of mine to someone who had run out. Another category of
people on board for which I had some concern were the elderly. I
did not know that many older folks were on the ship until we
landed in San-Pédro. I saw many elderly people and wondered how
they made it through the days. Perhaps they took lot more food on
board than I had taken on. I was judging other people's situation by
my own, thinking that because I had not taken much food on
board, so also others had not. I must have been mistaken. The
people around looked good and healthy and strong. Each time I
turned, I saw people preparing food or eating something. I was on a
regimented diet. I only ate once each day, and that was around
3:00pm. I witnessed true brotherliness and generosity among
Liberians aboard the ship. It was somewhat a big shift from what
was happening on the war front at home. Brothers were killing
brothers. The youth had total disregard for the elderly, and
everyone looked out for him/herself and their immediate family.
No one wanted to share anything. But that was reality on the main
land in Liberia, while the war was going on. No one could be
trusted; we were all unsure of the other person because of the
multitude of factions that were involved in the fighting, which
meant that anybody could be a fighter and a threat to another
person's life. But on the ship, the survival of one depended on and
affected the survival of the other. Each had to look out for the
other.

It's strange how circumstances can condition people's thinking
and behavior. From a health perspective, it made good sense to see

to the well being, of one another because the outbreak of an epidemic could have devastating effect in such an environment. Nobody wanted a sick person close by, especially, not in the congested situation as we were. I completely ran out of food on the fifth day. Everybody around me had also run out except one lady who had some raw rice and uncooked food.

By this time, we had developed acquaintances with most of the people within our section. Some of these acquaintances would go on to become lasting friends. Kadiatu Konteh, Solomon Lloyd and Charles Teah Bropleh are among some of the people within my section of the ship I remember very well. Solomon, I knew from my days at the Development Bank when he came to carry out banking transactions for the insurance company with which he worked as an agent. He sometimes frequented the bank, looking for clients and selling policies. As for Charles, I had known him for most of my life. We were relatives. Our parents were cousins and we grew up in the same neighborhood and attended school together. In fact, Charles was a part of the 20 that made the list. Kadiatu, I met on the ship along with her little daughter and fiancé. We talked each day and did things together.

One day when we had all run out of food – the long bread and biscuits received in San-Pédro—one of the ladies with raw rice decided to cook some. People were cooking on the ship. It was like a little village with smoke shooting in the air from points all over the deck. We managed to get some coal, borrowed a coal-pot and proceeded to cook. The only thing missing was water. We had drunk all the water we had received earlier, and so we tied a cloth on an empty container and drew some sea water. I was skeptical about this but it was the general consensus, so I followed along. The food was cooked but to our greatest disappointment, it was very salted from the sea water. Some people managed to eat but I couldn't eat so much salt. That was the beginning of my days without food for the rest of my journey. I don't know how many more days we had to go, but I knew I could stand it. Mentally, I was prepared for the time without food. Thanks to the spiritual practice of fasting, this was going to be a compulsory one for me. The first day was the most difficult for me. For the subsequent days, I had to muster the strength to stay alive. Those were the days that I really sat to think about the entire episode and my family and my life. What if my family had come with me? What if I died of hunger on the sea? The "what if" questions kept throbbing in my mind. I had no answer except the realization that life is what it is, and will happen in spite of what one thinks or does. But most importantly, I learned to understand not to fight against what one cannot change or have no control over. I learned to let go of my ego and opinion and desire to be judgmental based on mere perception. It can be faulty and the consequences irreversible.

The journey continued day and night, day and night—but with much uncertainty. The pace of the ship was slower than expected. Some attributed the slow pace to the prior leakage, while others thought it was a strategy to attract the attention and engage the Ghanaian authorities. Whatever it was, the journey was becoming unbearable with each passing day. The day of the week was unknown. I did not know if it was Monday or Wednesday or Saturday. I was just glad when each day came and I was alive to be counted among the living.

DEATH ON HIGH SEA

The passengers on the ship were a stunning replica of the Liberian demographics. They comprised of the elderly, pregnant women, mothers with babies and children, the young and old and the sick. People of all backgrounds, tribes and statuses: doctors, teachers, pastors, bankers, engineers, lawyers, the highly educated, the not so educated, and of course, some with no form of education at all. It was a true representation and reflection of our population: a population of a high level of illiteracy, and over 65% of youth and young adults. It could be easily said that the ratio of women to men on the ship was 2 to 1 or even 3 to 1. Every section of the ship was filled with more women than men.

Although strangers to one another and coming from various parts of the country, the passengers bonded well. We all had the one common fate of survival or death on the lonely sea. We looked out for one another. If anyone had some food, no matter how small, he or she would offer portions to those near by. If someone took ill, everyone showed concern, looking into their bags for whatever medication or first aid treatment that could help. We encouraged one another and raised the hopes of all that the journey would end peacefully and safe.

Before this journey, many of the people had never traveled by sea. They did not know what this experience would bring; nor did they know what to expect. And so, when people became seasick, it was a new experience, and, without proper medication or temporary treatment, every illness was a serious one. This was one of the most uncertain, no-option situations I'd ever known. Under normal circumstances, when a person gets sick, the family might have many options of going to either a hospital or clinic or to the

pharmacy; but in this case, there was nowhere to go and no one to
turn to. It was a dead-end situation. Much worse, the ship did not
even have first aid kits or emergency medical supplies for
treatment. Either your immune system fought and overcame the
illness or the illness overcame your immune system. Although it
did not occur in the section where I was, nor did I see it myself, we
did hear that a few deaths occurred on that dreadful journey. Later,
I read the Chicago Tribune report that "Three people have died on
ship since it left Liberia May 4, - a woman who bled uncontrollably
and two other people in an unexplained shooting. Disease is rife
among the passengers cooped up on board with only one toilet[13]." I
did not hear of shooting at any time during or after the journey.
Notwithstanding, I thought to myself, 'what happened to those
bodies if they did die? How were they disposed of? Were they kept
on the ship or were they thrown overboard into the ocean? What
would it be like for those people or their relatives or families?' Just
imagine - no funeral service and no family gathering; the
heartbreaking feeling of families and friends, knowing that they
would never have a memorial visit to a grave site of their loved
ones. How sad it would be if thrown into the sea! I could imagine
what would become of their bodies as they floated and drifted in
the roaring ocean. Fishes and sharks and other sea creatures would
feast on their bodies—plucking out eyes; eating fingers and toes;
biting on their ribs and fleshy parts. Bite after bite until their bodies
vanished and only bones and skulls remained. Somewhere along
some shore, on some beach, far from where their bodies were
dumped, their skulls and bones would appear. I could imagine what
pandemonium it would cause for some people in the communities
where these skeletal fragments would show-up. Depending on
where, the media institutions and the police would be on site to
report the mysterious find and to speculate as to who they might
have been, what might have happened, or what investigative break
they might have made into a murder case. This would make big
headlines while a family somewhere in a distance would be

grieving in silence about the demise of loved ones and a watery grave.

In spite of the rumors of deaths on the ship, the spirit of community arose as the brotherliness of Liberians emerged aboard the ship. It was strong and transcended tribal, social or economic barriers. It was a feeling as of the days of old, the kind I once knew when growing up; a feeling of care, love and togetherness. A feeling which suggests that while life may be uncertain, living demands that we build valuable relationships that foster communal living and reinforce concern for our fellowmen. We prayed for the souls of the dead, if any and for their families and the safety of the rest of the crew. We reassured one another that the Lord would uphold, protect and sustain us all beyond the current fear of the rumors being shared

In other instances of illnesses and near death situations, we prayed and encouraged individuals to keep their spirits upbeat; not to give in or give up; but to know that in time, it would all be well. We encouraged one another day after day to be strong; to keep the faith and to believe that God is able to heal us all of every sickness. As Christians and believers, that was a great way to witness to our faith. That was all we could do—turn things over to the Lord and trust God to do what was impossible to us, to heal. Death was not an option, faith was, but if death happened, we were there for one another. That was what it boiled down to, FAITH: faith in the absence of medicine or any form of care; faith to refuse death; faith to believe you can make it; and faith to hold on in failing health circumstances. While some have argued that faith is opposed to reason, proponents of faith argue that the proper domain of faith concerns questions which cannot be settled by evidence. We have the evidence to prove our faith: the men, women, boys and girls who made it to the shores and have survived to this very day. We celebrate their faith fight but most importantly, their restoration to health reassures us of the power and might of a God who promised healing to those who will believe.

I remember after couple of weeks of being in Ghana, a young man came up to me at an occasion and expressed how grateful he was for the courage we gave him in his life-and-death situation on the ship. He was one of the young men who had fallen ill. We did not know exactly what his illness was, but he was very ill and there was no medicine of any kind to give him. In his words, "I wanted to give up but you guys kept telling me there is much to life, and that I could make it." He stated that he ignored the pains and told himself how strong he was and that he was made for greatness, and believing in himself and the words of comfort, his spirit became stronger than the pains. "This kept me from day to day till we arrived in Takoradi," he testified. His story, like many others, is reflective of the general characteristic of Liberians and our ability to function past trials, tribulations, frustrations and disappointments.

Our journey continued with no idea of what could be the next challenge.

"The downpour was heavy;
the breeze got stronger,
the waves were rough, and the ship
began to rock from side to side."

ONE STORMY NIGHT: A NEAR DEATH EXPERIENCE

Something was peculiar about the trip. In the day time the ship travelled slowly and took for hours to cover short distances. Some days it looked as though the ship was just still – sitting in one place; and then, each night it took off with great speed. You could hear the high whining noise of the engine and feel the ship gracefully gliding through the dark waters. I could not understand the difference in the movement of the ship from daytime to nighttime.

In the human world, nothing seems to happen for nothing. In other societies where the approach to scientific experimentation is very strong, people insist upon relying on scientific evidence. Conversely, were scientific experimentation is not very strong; people tend to rely on superstition. This is true, for example, in several regions of Africa. Liberia, sadly, is part of that category. And so, with the apparent misfortune of the ship, rumors began circulating that the ship was possessed—demonically possessed; that the crew intended to make sacrifice of the entire ship and occupants aboard. According to the rumors, that was why the ship sped so aggressively at night, but slower in the daytime. I dismissed the thought as mere superstition because of my faith and belief in the power of God. I had been taught, had learned and experienced firsthand, how important it is to believe in God than in superstition or voodoo or black power.

All the while, the weather had been excellent, with the sun blazingly hot every day. Under ordinary circumstances, the rain would occasionally fall, but, so far, we had sailed without any incident of bad weather. What a blessing! I just couldn't imagine

the disaster it would be with thousands of people on the deck in a
heavy rain; "a great uproar," I reasoned to myself. But the weather
had been good so far. I attributed it to prayers from people on
board as well as to relatives and friends, who I am sure, had been
praying for the war in Liberia to end, and particularly for the *Bulk
Challenge* voyage.

I looked forward to night time because the air would be cool
and the temperature mild. It was a time to recover some lost
energy in anticipation of the next day's journey. The scorching heat
of the sun was becoming more and more unbearable with each
additional day of sailing. My blue and white stripy shirt had faded.
The complexion of my arm was becoming darker from the
compulsory tanning from the sun. The hours of the day seemed
longer; it felt like 40 instead of 24 hours. I couldn't wait for the
night to come. I watched as the sunset glistened upon the horizon
with such glow and beauty.

Aside from the ship on the sea, the sky above my head, and the
hardwood deck beneath my feet, a sense of calm engulfed me
whenever evening came. I was reminded by the words of Nicholas
Sparks in The Notebook, "Dusk is just an illusion because the sun is
either above the horizon or below it." And that meant that day and
night are linked in a way that some things cannot be one without
the other yet they cannot exist at the same time. Indeed, my best
time of day was nearing and something inside of me told me it
would be worth my wait. Unfortunately, what came was
unexpected, unwelcomed and unacceptable. It happened without
warning.

The night was still young; the breeze was blowing and
becoming cooler by the minute, but the flickering lights of the stars
were fading away; and with each disappearance, the night grew
darker and cooler; much cooler than days before. It wasn't very
long when I felt a sting on my arm, only to discover it was one of
those big drops of rain that fall with such force that it hurts like
you've been stung by a baby bee. Then another drop fell on my

forehead, and another, and another; and they came even faster. A downpour appeared imminent. What would we do? What would happen? How much of it would we receive? How long would it last? These were the thoughts that crowded my mind. Not once did I think of the wind and its effect when it rains. Although I had traveled by ship before, I had never experienced rain on an open-deck. So, I did not know what to expect. I knew we would definitely get wet and stay wet for a while, but the thought of what effect extra water on the deck would have on the ship's ability to stay afloat, squeezed a silent chilling unwanted fear into my heart. And before we could think through and circumstance, the rain came gushing down, as if heaven's water faucet had broken loose and all of its reserve was falling in one place at once—on our ship. The downpour was heavy; the breeze got stronger, the waves were rough, and the ship began to rock from side to side. It was a storm no one anticipated; a storm that caught us all by surprise. For a moment I thought we would all be buried in the depth of the angry ocean. Too many people as food for one night, I thought. But my wandering mind could not ease the fear now raging on the ship; it could not ease my own fear. Gazing around the deck, it seemed like everything was in slow motion. I watched the reactions of the people beside me. Despite the rain and the fear that we could be in much greater danger than the previous leakage, their faces remained blank, seemingly unaffected and composed.

It was clear thatwe were in a storm. Not knowing what to do, or how to feel, I realized I too was a passive onlooker, helpless and vulnerable. I was no different from the people sitting next to me.

I was not even sure I could swim if the ship was to capsize. I became absent-minded in the fear of not knowing what to do. The ship was rocking to near overturning. People were tossed from side to side and place to place, each holding on to the next to keep some balance, and from falling overboard. It seemed that several forces of nature were acting against us: the wind, the waves, and the rain. It was a war of nature against man, at the detriment of man, and man without the ability to fight back or protect himself. What a tough spot to be in! Screams were ringing in the air from all over the ship. Not too many people took notice of the tarpaulin— a kind of cover sheeting—that was placed over the ship as protection from the sun. But someone did and shouted: "The tarpaulin! Loose the tarpaulin!" Although it was placed in select areas over the ship's deck, the effect of the wind on the tarpaulin was felt on the entire ship. As the wind blew, it swept into the tarpaulin, filling it with a sudden powerful puff that almost lifted the ship, and with the dashing of the waves against the ship, the ship was rocked from side to side. A group of men tried to make their way to the points where the tarpaulin was hooked to the ship. It took hours to reach those points, for each time a group got closer, the ship twisted again and everyone would go swaying in other directions. But we all realized that the only way to stabilize the ship was to cut the tarpaulin off at the points where it was attached to the deck. So all efforts were put into reaching those points and untying or cutting off those knots.

We struggled and struggled, bouncing off, and swinging back, falling off our feet and hanging back on to the rope. When the wind calmed for a few minutes, we seized the opportunity to take down the tarpaulin. But the struggle had just begun; untying the knots was even more difficult than reaching to the knots or anchor points. The knots had been tightened from the force of the wind and the movement of the ship. It could not be unloosed easily with hands. "Get a knife, get a knife and cut the rope," someone shouted from across the deck. So we sought for someone who had a knife or any sharp instrument. But finding one was just as hard since all our belongings were moved around so much during the shifts and tossing of the ship. By the time the knives were found, the wind had begun blowing again. I remember quite clearly when the knot at our end was cut. The ship was leaning on the side and as the knot was cut, the entire ship swung back in place with a great force.

What a relief it was! "Oh thank God," I said to myself. This was a near death experience and I could think of nothing else but landing ashore and getting off that ship. The destination did not matter to me anymore; wherever would just fine with me. I wanted to get off. The wind continued to blow, and the rain continued to fall, but the tossing of the ship had ceased.

It seems like the thought of death brings out man's natural animal instinct for survival. I learned a great lesson that night: that when the common interest of a people is threatened, the natural response is to work together against that threat. That was the case with us that night. We all worked to get the job done, to stabilize the ship, and the result was beneficial to all. But what must be remembered and which is even more imperative is the realization that each person must perceive the situation as a threat not just to himself/ herself, but a threat to and against all. It is the "we" and/or "us" factor that makes the difference. It doesn't have to be a threat, but if we can perceive a situation—any situation—in a communal sense, then working together to find the solution can be much easier. This is a lesson we can all draw from—whether in politics, civic or religious situations, we can affect change for the good of all mankind when we, not if we, but when we collaborate with all our efforts toward a common end. Our families can be stronger, our communities can benefit, and our world can be a better place.

The rain stopped, the stars began to slowly reappear, one by one, lighting up the night sky. The wind calmed and the sail of the ship was smooth as if nothing had ever happened. We searched the ship—quarter by quarter—to make sure we did not lose anyone during the stormy episode. And certainly, all was accounted for, thankfully. Soaked and dripping with water, cold and chilling, I returned to my spot on the stair to the cabin, trying to make sense of what had just happened. How long had it lasted? I really didn't know and don't believe anyone knew. We were so consumed with the fight to stay alive that time was the least of our concern.

However long it lasted, it seemed like it went on for hours. I tried to sleep afterwards but being wet was so uncomfortable that I just sat there with my head on my knees. Not many people slept earlier. And perhaps, nobody slept at all. throughout the night, conversations could be heard all around me. I joined one of those talk sessions till we began to see the night clear into day.

One thing was certain during that near-death experience: we were united in an effort to save our lives, and it worked. The team-work and unity in the effort to untie the tarpaulin spoke volume as to the essence of "community." That night, I saw team effort at work and it saved our lives and the lives of many.

I say "community" because community comes in many forms, shapes and sizes. Each of us, no matter where we find ourselves, belongs to one kind or the other – whether it be a hamlet, village, town or city, a national or the big encompassing international community. In addition to "size" as a principal basis of differentiation, it is important to note that other pertinent attributes such as desired or appropriate sets of values, intents, beliefs, resources, preferences, needs, risks and other conditions are crucial and common to a community. They affect the identity of the participants and the degree of cohesiveness among them. If I should summarize, I would say that the idea of community simply come down to the joint positive, supportive activities of individuals who share a vested interest. Whether your vested interest is in the well-being of your neighborhood or extends to the well-being of the global community, your survival is a function of the survival factors of the greater whole. We, on the *Bulk Challenge* embodied every definition of community: our interests, hopes and fates were all intertwined on a ship that began with a "crack in the hatch."

In the case of Liberia, if Liberians can look positively on the things that make us truly Liberians – all the interests and values, our food and unique style, our beliefs, resources and hospitality – and put aside the differences that persist on inserting a wedge among us, we can become one of the greatest nations on planet earth. It is not that we can't live peaceably with each other, but we seem to be a people who have been robbed, by fate, of the quality of leadership needed to take us to the necessary level of devout patriotism and nationalism. The war, from which we were fleeing, was a classic example of the result of poor leadership. Those who orchestrated the so-called "war of redemption" had ill-informed and misdirected the vault of our future–the youths–into believing the wrong intent of the war. They preyed on the ignorance of the youth, took advantage of their innocence and vulnerability and robbed them of the opportunity to grow up as children into and through the various stages of life; like we did, in our time. "Like we did?" Yes, like we did. Growing up, our interactions with others was void of the concerns about or for tribes. We played together, studied together, hung out together, visited and stayed over at one another's homes, but never once—to the best of my recollection—did the difference of our tribes interfere with our relationships or interactions. Now, with the infusion of the tribal element within and among a highly illiterate population, the dynamics of engagements and human relations has changed forever. Tribal issues and concerns will remain a factor for continuous reconciliation, peace building, conflict resolution and national development for years and generations to come.

A great lesson is here to be learned from this experience. It is that Liberians and all peoples of the world, can live together in harmony and bond, and appreciate the value of our differences if we focus on our common interest—national development for all. When we work to elevate the least among us, through education and training and other forms of empowerment, we are, in effect, increasing the value of our people which alternately increases the value of our community. When we seek to ensure that all peoples have access to health care and treatment for preventable illnesses, we are seeking to extend the lifespan of our people and additionally increasing the capability of the population to sustain the efforts of national development. When we make decisions for political leadership based on who is best qualified, prepared and ready to serve, rather than stick to individuals based on tribal or other affiliations, then we are working together to grow our nation and advance the policy prescriptions that invariably grow every member of the society. These are possible endeavors, achievable with structured policies, dedicated leadership and enforceable laws.

So where do we begin? It must begin with each of us taking actions to do the right thing. As William H. Johnsen puts it, "If it is to be, it is up to me." This is the approach that each of us must take. It simply means assuming responsibility, taking charge and avoiding the temptation of waiting for someone else to do it. When each of us begin to appropriate ourselves in taking responsibility we eventually end up working together for the common good of all, growing to becoming "ONE" from "MANY." In other words, all Liberians must see LIBERIA as belonging to all Liberians and not to a few. This is when our mentality of "I", "me" and "myself" will be changed to "we" and "our" and "us". For, it is when "we" work together, in spite of our differences and tribal linkages, that we can consolidate our ideas, shift our thoughts for the better and put forth our best effort for the benefit of all.

A VISION OR WHAT?

Have you ever heard of voodoo, juju or black magic? Do you believe in superstition? Do you know or have heard about witchcraft or witch-doctor? Some people believe such powers do not exist, whereas others observe that such denial is a huge mistake: witchcraft and witch-doctors do exist. However, as familiar as they all may seem to some, there are vast differences among them all. Juju comes from the traditional African religion popularly known as voodoo. In juju the mode of operation is spiritual. Because of Christianity, Islam, etc. in these days, most people don't believe in juju powers. Juju is very popular in Benin (the motherland of voodoo) and also Haiti, but not just Africans. Even some Native Americans such as the Cherokees and the Apaches believe in juju powers. Although juju may sound strange to some people, voodoo is part of our (African) culture and traditions. In other words, Africans cannot throw away voodoo. Voodoo is part of Africa. The difference between juju and voodoo (the traditional African religion) is that the traditional African religion or voodoo mostly helps people unlike juju which mostly harms people. Voodoo practitioners are mostly herbalists and wise men who use combination of herbs, barks of trees, etc. to cure diseases. Some get the knowledge from ancestral spirits and the lesser gods they worship. Juju performers on the other hand use strange objects like the skull of dead animals, human skulls, etc. to perform juju powers which mostly harms people. In some situations, when they (juju practitioners) know they cannot help, instead of telling people straight away, they demand for even more insane items that are impossible to find; like the front tooth of a lion, the sperm of a dinosaur, etc. They make such impossible requests to place the burden on the client and establish a basis to justify their inability to perform what they were asked to perform. For example, one might say, "Well, I cannot do this for you because you failed to bring the sperm of a cobra."

In all, if not most of Africa, traditional medicine men (sometimes women) are common—particularly, throughout sub-Saharan Africa in almost every good-sized village, where they practice as herbalists as well as spiritual advisers. Some have better reputations than others, and some are better than others at curing certain ailments. People shop around just like anyone in the developed world might do when looking for a psychiatrist or chiropractor.

The belief in and the practice of magic has been present since the earliest human cultures and continues to have an important religious and medicinal role in many cultures today. Magic is often viewed with suspicion in some societies, and therefore is sometimes practiced in isolation and secrecy.

The concept of magic as a category separate from religion first appeared in Judaism, which derided as magic the practices of pagan worship designed to appease and receive benefits from gods other than Yahweh. Hank Hanegraaff argues that magic is in fact "...*a largely polemical concept that has been used by various religious interest groups either to describe their own religious beliefs and practices or—more frequently—to discredit those of others.*"[14] In non-scientific societies, perceived magical attack is an idea sometimes employed to explain personal or societal misfortune. In the historical, traditional context, this is often termed witchcraft or sorcery, and the perceived attackers "witches" or "sorcerers." Known members of the community may be accused of being witches, or the witches may be perceived as supernatural, non-human entities. On the other hand, witchcraft (also called *witchery* or *spellcraft*) is the use of magical faculties, most commonly for religious, divinatory or medicinal purposes. This may take many forms, depending on cultural context. However, the concept of witchcraft as harmful is often treated as a cultural ideology providing a scapegoat for human misfortune.[15]

Africans, for example, know that there are spiritual forces and powers that exist and are at work in this world, and we have heard many stories of demonic activities and spiritual wickedness. But as a Christian I have always believed that the power of God is greater than any power in the world. This is not to say that other powers don't exist but that they become powerless when you stand on your faith and conviction of the power and presence of God.

As has been stated, the *Bulk Challenge* was traveling closer along the shores and as such we could clearly see houses in the day time and lights of those houses along the shores, at night. I had a particular spot on the ship where I spent the day and night. It was the stairway that led from the deck into the ship itself. During the day, it was my sitting spot and my living room from where I conversed with others. I barely moved from this spot for fear that someone would take my place. Each night I would turn to rest my head on the stair above where I sat, and sleep. Directly behind and above the stairs was a window to one of the cabins. I had been in that cabin before and had seen the arrangements in the room. But one night as I turned to rest my head, I saw what could only be explained as a ritual being performed. The room now looked wider then I knew it to be. There was one bed toward the wall on my left. On the bed was a woman— very huge woman. Only her legs were shown and her upper part was covered with a traditional "lappa."

In Liberia, the word refers to loin or waistcloth, especially the one worn by women. "Lappas," especially those which women wear on special occasions, are usually bright, colorful and beautifully patterned fabric. Often, a lappa measures about two yards of fabric.

This night, as I turned to rest my head, I saw five other women lying on the floor; they were all half-naked except for the under pants they wore. They bowed in a certain way and made motions as if in a choreographic dance group or cultural troupe. These five

women looked like they were worshipping the woman on the bed.
At one time, they fell on their knees with their hands stretched
upward, palm facing the ceiling; then together they pressed their
faces to the floor and lay flat on the ground with all heads together
but bodies stretched out in different directions. I don't know how
long these women stayed in that posture, but it seemed like
forever. At first, I thought I was asleep and dreaming, but as I recall,
I was not sleepy when I turned away from the folks I was
conversing with in our section of the ship. We did this every night -
just converse to pass the night away. Those nights were long with
no activity to occupy our time. But this night was different. What I
saw stunned me. I turned away from the room and turned back
toward the room, but the women were still there. I couldn't
understand what was going on with those women and all their
various movements around the lady on the bed. It looked as if they
were performing some sort of ritual, but I really couldn't tell if it
was a vision, a dream of something demonic. So, I started praying
silently. My thoughts were consumed in prior information I heard
about the captain and his crew's attempt to take the ship to Nigeria
to make sacrifices of the passengers. I began to prayer what
Pentecostals called "the warfare prayer." Silently, I started casting
out demons, binding the devil, speaking the blood of Jesus over the
ship and proclaiming that no plans of the enemy would succeed. I
prayed for as long as I watched the situation in the room.

Then I turned to look behind at the folks still having general
conversation. I wanted to call one of my buddies and prayer partner
to join me, but as I turned back to the window, the room was
completely dark. I could not see anything at all. I just couldn't
understand what had just happened. The next morning, I called the
two brothers with whom I prayed daily – Solomon Lloyd, now
Rev. Lloyd, and Charles Teah Bropleh – and explained to them
what I saw the night before. We prayed about it and decided to go
into the ship and into the cabin behind the step. We discovered that
the room was far from what I had seen and shared with them.

There were two beds, one on each side of the room, with a coffee table mounted on the floor between the two beds. There was no indication that the table had been moved and/or replaced. It was clear it was a permanent fixture since the building of the ship. We concluded that what I had seen was a vision or dream or a revelation that God wanted me to see, so as to reinforce our prayer vigilance. We went back to our individual spots on the ship and, like I said, we continued to pray vigilantly. Our prayer took a new turn. It was more warfare then just prayer for grace and safety. We concluded that the ship was possessed, and that therefore there was much work for us believers in order to show that God is greater, and that no force can stand against the children of God.

In fact, it is clearly written in Scriptures that, *"no weapons formed against you shall prosper – Isaiah 54:17 (NIV)"*— It is also indicated in John 8:8 (NIV) that *"... we are more than conquerors in Christ Jesus who strengthens us ...."* The authority that believers have is so great that it can change any situation for the good. It may be a plan of the enemy for the worse to happen, but the power of God in the children of God, through prayer, can change all things around. This is what makes knowing God so great. Believers know that they have power and when they stand, they don't stand alone. Angels and archangels stand with them and fight on the believers' behalf. Indeed, all that I thought I saw that night increased our prayer regiment. Each morning began with worship. On a lonely sea, on a leaking ship, going against the wind and rain, and forces unknown, that was the only weapon we had—prayer.

"…..as we sailed into the harbor, two gunboats
escorted us; one on the left
and the other on the right—
just as Charles had prophesized –
escorting us instead of shooting at us."

LAST LEG OF THE JOURNEY

One morning, we awoke to the beauty of a city stretched out along the Atlantic Ocean. As the morning became clearer and as we got closer, we saw two gun boats approaching our ship. Great joy welled up in our hearts. Oh, what a good day. We thought the boats were a friendly welcome team, coming to take us to the harbor, but we were mistaken. As the boats drew nearer, they ordered that the captain turn the ship around and leave the Ghanaian territorial waters. The Ghanaian news had reported an exchange of gunfire aboard the Bulk Challenge – but this was untrue. The captain turned the ship around and went back into the ocean.

The next day, we saw the ship going back toward the Takoradi Port. We were all filled with joy, thinking the Ghanaian Government had considered our plight and called the ship back; or so I thought. But no, we saw the two gun boats approach again. We heard a voice over the loud speaker saying, "Turn back and do not come any further, or else you will be shot at." This time, to demonstrate their seriousness not to allow us entry, they shot about four rounds into the air. The feeling of joy turned to fear as cries rang out from every angle of the ship. We thought the gun boats were shooting at us. If they did, the ship would have sunk and many, if not all of us, would have perished. I must admit, at that moment, I was just as afraid as anyone else on the ship. People were shouting and crying all over the ship. I was mesmerized. In the midst of the shouting and crying, weeping and wailing, it took the courage of Charles Tieh Bropleh, to stand up and silence everyone. What he did and said re-awaken my own sense of awareness of the fact that no situation, no difficulty, and no condition is beyond God's ability to change. As the noise quieted down, he began to speak, prophetically. He declared, *"the Lord is on our side; He has brought us thus far, and He will see us through to the end of this journey. And I want you to know that the very gunboats that are threatening us are the very gunboats that will escort us into safety. So don't be afraid. Have faith and know our God is not dead, He is alive."* And he began to prayer. As he did, the ship slowly turned away from the direction of the city and was headed back into the sea. No later, someone raised the song, "God's not dead, He is alive" and we all began to sing.

We were busy singing so much so that we never noticed what occurred while our attention was away from the gunboats. Then after nearly an hour or more, we heard the voice again over the loud speaker. We all stopped singing to get the message, thinking it was a reinforcement of the original message to leave Ghanaian territorial waters. But no, it was a call to the captain to turn the ship back and pull into the harbor at Takoradi. At first, we thought we were misunderstanding the message, but the speaker repeated it several times, and as the ship turned facing the city, we knew for sure that we were finally disembarking in Ghana. But most importantly, as we sailed into the harbor, the very gunboats that had fired those warning shots, were the gunboats escorting the Bulk Challenge into the harbor – one on the left and the other, on the right—just as Charles had prophesized; escorting us instead of shooting at us. This was one of the many manifestations of the power of God, honoring His word. It was a testimony to the fact that it takes only one person's faith to make a difference for many. Indeed, *"the prayer of a righteous person is powerful and effective – James 5:16 (NIV)"*. At that moment, it was like seeing the spoken word, come alive. This single manifestation reinforced my faith in God. With the gunboats on each side of the ship, escorting us into the harbor, we exploded into singing, even louder, *"God's not dead, He is alive."* Charles broke up in a serious prayer of thanksgiving and gratitude and we prayed along with him in agreement.

Inch by inch our ship made its way into the harbor of the City of Sekondi-Takoradi. The Sekondi-Takoradi Metropolitan District is one of the eighteen (18) districts of Ghana in the Western Region. It comprises the twin cities of Sekondi and Takoradi which comprise the capital of the Western Region of Ghana, and an industrial and commercial center. The chief industries in Sekondi-Takoradi are timber, plywood, shipbuilding and railroad repair, and crude oil. Sekondi, older and larger, was the site of Dutch Fort Orange in 1642 and English Fort Sekondi in 1682. It prospered from a railroad built in 1903 to transport mineral and timber resources. Takoradi was the site of Dutch Fort Witsen in 1665 and has an important deep-water seaport. During World War II, Takoradi Air Base was an important staging point for British aircraft destined for Egypt. The cities combined in 1946. Sekondi-Takoradi has plenty of beaches; however, they are not a major tourist attraction. Many beaches are also found to the west of Takoradi, with small resorts such as Fanta's Folly, The Hideout, and Green Turtle Lodge. The city is currently named (although not officially) as the Oil City of Ghana due to the massive discovery of oil in the western region, and has attracted massive migration from people all over the world[16].

As the ship prepared to anchor, making room for the passengers to disembark, people came from far and wide to see the ship that had been stranded on sea for many days. They lined up along the dock and waved joyfully. Vehicles reeled into the port area; trucks and SUVs with the emblems of the United Nations (UN) and Red Cross. There were military and police cars as well. It was a wonderful site to see help finally arrived as various teams converged to deliver services and to address the needs of the people from the Bulk Challenge.

"….And we formed lines, as directed,
to be registered.
Several registration tables
were clearly marked.
Volunteers from
Red Cross
and government
agencies assisted with
the registration process"

The place got crowded. The ship finally reached the dock and was anchored. Passengers were told to remain on board until the authorities on the ground gave the command to get off. The sun was blazingly hot and we were anxious to get down, but we sat and sat for many minutes, if not hours. Finally, from the ground came instructions from one of the authorities as to how we were to proceed once we got off the ship. Government authorities and humanitarian teams had set up reception areas, registration tables and emergency stations.

The first group of people to be taken off the ship were those identified as sick or with medical conditions, and needed special attention. The severely sick were taken in ambulance directly to nearby hospitals and/or clinics, while others were treated by the Red Cross Emergency Team in the stations set up at the arrival site. The rest of the passengers were directed to form lines to be registered. Several registration tables were clearly marked.

Unlike the Ghanaians, we, Liberians, are not used to organized line systems at all. So it became a rushing, pushing, shuffling process – each person wanting to be ahead on the line. It was so chaotic that the police had to get involved to establish order. It reminded me of my days in college whenever we went for registration. We had to form lines according to last names (A to F; G to L; M to R and S to Z). It was always a tug-of-war—people cutting the lines; pushing and shuffling; and even fighting, thereby disrupting the process. When the Ghanaian authorities got involved, in no time, the disorderliness changed. Everyone conformed to the instructions of the authorities and the lines at the registration tables became organized and orderly. It was emphatically stated that anyone found disrupting a line would be held back to the end of the process. No one wanted to be that person, so everyone conformed to the process. The sun was hot; much hotter than in Liberia. And although the process seemed long, dreary and tiring, it was actually smoother than expected, because with the order came efficiency, effectiveness and maximum use of everyone's time.

The orderliness of the lines taught me an important lesson; that organization, structure and systems save time. Order makes a process easier. One by one, we were registered. We gave our basic information - name, date of birth, sex, etc., and they gave each person a number and directed us to another booth where an emergency kit containing band aid, water, a pack of biscuits and a blanket, was given. Then we took the number to any of the buses or military trucks and boarded. When all was said and done, the convoy headed off for the destination that would become our place of refuge.

It was an abandoned school campus with one building in a little village called Essipon, located on the outskirts of Sekondi. That was where we were taken. There is nothing much to be said about Essipon. Driving from Sekondi to Essipon, the town looked deserted. Apart from rock crushing as a major economic activity in the area, most of the inhabitants sustain themselves by engaging in subsistence farming, particularly corn farming, and fishery[17]. Their crops were sold on market days to people from other villages and the city. There were no stores, businesses, clinics or offices. Residents had to travel to the nearby town or city center for most of everything—school, market, hospital and other businesses. It had a single-lane dirt road that passed through the village and onward to the next.

The campus on which we would reside was a technical institute, but it didn't seem to be operational at the time. It contained one main building with several class rooms, offices, and a vocational workshop at the back of the school. In the front of the school was a soccer field. Could it be that the authorities did not want to be bother with us, that we were taken to a place so remote? We had no choice. Being in Essipon was better than being on that ship, and on the water. More importantly, it was far better than being in Liberia under the sounds of guns shooting and bullets flying.

We got off the busses and trucks in the front of the school building. Women with young children and babies, as well the elderly, were ushered inside the school building, while the rest of us were left standing in the school yard. Emergency relief packets were distributed to us according to the registration done in Takoradi. Each packet included a tent with all its pitching fixtures, and two wool sheets. Somehow, my group managed to secure a second packet (will not say how).   Later, we scouted around the school grounds for a suitable spot, and there we constructed our tent. Solomon, Charles and I got to work and built it. The work was so neatly done that one would have thought we were professional tent builders. In a sense, we were, because later, many people called on us for help, and throughout the night we went on helping others set up their tents.

The meal was prepared at our refugee camp by volunteers who had come to work at the camp. Again we had to line up to get served corn cereal and bread. By the end of the night, we were so very exhausted that we slept like babies without noticing we were sleeping on the ground. When morning came, we were gathered in small groups and schooled on the camp rules. One of the rules was to get a pass before leaving the camp. In the building were offices for the Red Cross, UNHCR and the Military.

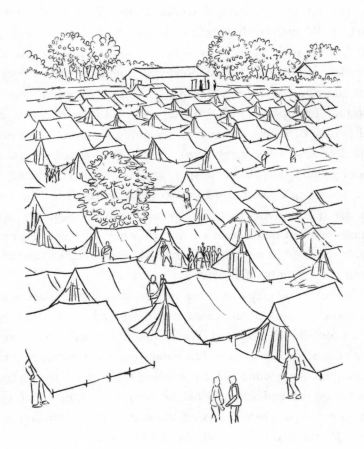

"Emergency relief
Packets were distributed to us according to the
registration done in Takoradi. Each packet
included a tent with all its
pitching fixtures, and two wool sheets. We
constructed tents and filled the area of the field, as
our new dwelling place."

There were two main entrances to the campus and both were guided by soldiers to ensure protection of the refugees as well as making sure no one left to go into town unofficially. Our luggage, we were told, would be brought to the camp later. Sekondi was the closest city center to the camp. It was approximate 20 minutes away.

Walking around the camp, I began to meet people who I never knew were on the ship. Sometimes I ran into them; at other times, they spotted me first and called. I just didn't believe my eyes. I saw a family who were close friends to my parents. Can't say their names at this time, but I was so glad to see them; it had been several years since I last saw them. We talked about the old days. They asked about my parents. Their children and I grew up together and went to school together. As a matter of fact, my best friend, growing up, was the only son they ever had. "Tonia" was his name. I remembered when he passed in 1979; it was the greatest painful experience of my youthful life —an experience I never thought I would overcome. It took years for the pain of his death to heal. Every time I visited my parents in Buchanan, I made it my duty to stop by and speak to his parents. Eventually, these visits became increasingly difficult for me as every visit brought back painful memories of our time spent together and the plans we shared. He was a brilliant, talented and skillful young man. I assured them that while in Ghana, I would be around and available to assist them whenever they needed me to do something for them.

I saw a whole lot of people, I can't even begin to name: a workmate of mine, Gartoun George; a church mate who was also my former professor, Prof. K. Moses Nagbe; a high school buddy, Anthony McDaniels; a prominent community member, Mr. James Davis; Hon. Gayah Fahnbulleh; Prince Jallabah, and many others. In addition to people I knew, I also met and made some new acquaintances and friends— such as Kadiatu Konteh, Sam Weedor and Theophylus During.

We were not too comfortable with the area where our tent was and so on the third day, we found a spot at the back of the school building, and there we set up our second tent and relocated. It was a much better area. We had lots of fun on that side of the building. We even named our area Nashville and one of the walkways, Dorcas Avenue. I became the Governor of Nashville. Those were memorable times of my stay at Essipon and life as a refugee.

Several civic and religious groups visited the camp on the second day to see what assistance they could give in addition to what was provided by the UNHCR and Red Cross. Church leaders from specific denominations came to look for members of their denominations, bringing clothing, food, beddings and even money. Pastors of other local churches came to offer comfort and hope, and extended invitation to their churches.

The first trip Solomon, Charles and I made out of the camp was to honor the invitation of one of the local pastors. We attended the morning worship and had a warm welcome. The service was great and we made the church our place of worship. On our second visit, the pastor invited us to dinner at his home. From our conversation he discovered that we too were students of the Bible. We shared our testimonies, and we prayed. The entire congregation not only empathized with us, but also respected us much. We encouraged others to go with us and they did. Various denominations began holding worship services on the camp. Initially, it was an interdenominational worship service and everybody joined in and thanked God, week after week. It was great because it reflected unity as everybody came together. But when the leadership of these denominational churches encouraged their members to start services that would reflect the denomination's worship structure, practices and tradition, it created a kind of division again, and resulted in several worship services going on at the same time every Sunday. Some groups even erected churches. In spite of this, one of the spiritual exercises I enjoyed the most was the early morning prayer-time. At 5am every morning Charles, Solomon, myself, and a few other men and women would assemble at a particular part of the camp to pray for an hour, or sometimes an hour and the half. It was so refreshing; we prayed for the war and destruction in Liberia to cease; for our situation on the camp; against sickness; we thank God each day for His faithfulness toward us; for the government and people of Ghana; for provision and for good health. Each day I left the prayer session spiritually charged and fulfilled.

On the day that the luggage from the ship arrived, I was filled with mixed emotions, excitement and anger: excited that the things had arrived but angry that they were wet and possibly damaged. It took several trips and a full day to complete the delivery of our belongings. And then a week passed and we still had not heard when we were going to identify and take delivery of our things. It was what we were waiting for to leave and go to Buduburam. The day finally came and announcement was made regarding the process. The registration list would be used and individuals would be called according to heads of households. It was a long process. Many luggages looked similar, and because they were wet, names were erased from the name-tags, such that identifying and claiming a luggage became difficult. Several days passed before we were called. I walked around the field looking for my suitcase. I was not particular about the clothes but I had my university diploma and other important documents and credentials that I didn't want to lose. When I signed off on my suitcase, and opened it, the sea water had wet and damaged many of the clothes. I was pulling off a shirt and right in my hands it tore into pieces. Piece by piece, I took the clothes from the suitcase till I found the folder that contained the documents. I opened it. Of course, papers were stuck together and pulling them apart further destroyed them. Ink on my diploma had spill over it; it looked bad. Solo and Charles found their things as well and we were ready any day to leave. By this time, leaving the camp was not as difficult as it was in the beginning. We left when we wanted to and came when we wanted to. The officers were familiar with us; some of them knew us personally. Some individuals from Buduburam visited the camp and through them, we made initial contact with our relatives at the camp.

Our experience in Sekondi was a good one. We made many acquaintances in Ghana—with folks in the church we attended as well as people on the street. It was a survival strategy that paid off well in our favor. One of the friendships we cherished the most was with some women who sold food on the street in front of their home. It was well prepared and very tasty. My favorites were "Banku" and "Watchen." Many of us became good friends with these food mongers. In the end, we had heartwarming preferential treatment as customers. For example, instead of sitting on the side of the street to eat, like most buyers did, our food was put aside, and taken in the house or on the porch where we sat in comfortable chairs and ate. Their family knew us and we were welcome any time. Sometimes when they were not selling, we would visit and sit and talk together. They were great hosts. When Solo and I decided to relocate from the camp, it was at their place that we took our belongings a couple of days before we actually left.

Essipon was a place where people did more walking rather than using automobiles to get around. Hence, it was often difficult to get a vehicle to travel to Essipon. After all, if public transport drivers did, it was highly unlikely that drivers would find passengers to take back to the city. But with the presence of the camp, a transport market was created, and cabs and buses flocked into the area daily, up to 10:00pm. Beyond 10pm, anyone wishing to return to the camp had to charter a vehicle or simply choose to walk longer distances like the rest of the people in Essipon.

Our first experience with the vehicle shortage was a tough one. We had stayed all day in Sekondi and later went to Takoradi to hang out. By the time we were ready to return home, it was way past 11:30pm. All attempts to charter a cab proved futile. That night, we had to walk back to the camp –Solo, Charles and I, as well as others we had met at the parking station in Sekondi. We set out and began the 16-mile walk back to the camp. It was a long one but we talked all the way during the journey so that we did not feel the distance. It was therapeutic in a sense because we found out that we could walk the distance and did not have to rush coming back to the camp. Many days following that night, we would stay in Takoradi and walk home when we got ready. We were no more conditioned by the lack of vehicles after 11pm. We just hung out in Takoradi until we were tired or ready to go to the camp. It's like what folks say: "Every condition, every problem eventually brings along its own remedy."

With our luggage in our possession, we began planning to leave the camp to go to Buduburam. Part of the plan was to get our things out of the camp to a location within Sekondi, so that when we decided to leave, we could walk in plain daylight with our hands swinging and no one would know we were leaving. We discussed leaving our things with our friends in Sekondi, and they agreed. But we did not take the things immediately; at least we knew we had a place if we had to. When rumor spread around the camp that the refugees were to be transferred to a location further west, we accelerated our plans and smocked our suitcases out of the camp. That night, we took them to our friends in Sekondi. It was late when we got there and could not walk back to the camp (it was only Solo and I), so we went over to the church we attended. We knew that one of the members slept there. We knocked on the door, announced ourselves, and he opened the door. We explained that we could not walk back to the camp. He was more than willing for us to share the night with him. So, we slept at the church and returned to the camp the next morning.

LEAVING TAKORADI

The day came for our camp at Essipon to be relocated further west. The new camp was in a western area known as Sanzule. We boarded the bus early. It was somewhat sad to be leaving Essipon. As we left, Solomon and I agreed that we would return after we settled at Sanzule, and make our way to the Buduburam Camp where we had friends and where the community was more hospitable. The travel to Sanzule was a long journey. We arrived in Sanzule at about 4:30pm. The new site was a coconut plantation. One could tell that the place was still being prepared, as some yellow machines were still on the site clearing trees to make way for tents to be built. Also, there was no electricity. We were warned not to pick or eat any of the coconuts that fell from the trees. Rumors had it that if anyone did, he/she would die. How true was the rumor? We could not tell. But Sanzule was a scary looking place. We wanted to return that very night, but we couldn't, because there was no vehicle traveling from that side of town back to Sekondi. The area was so remote that transport vehicles usually traveled there from morning hours up to 4pm. Vehicles that were seen after 4pm usually stayed overnight to take the early morning passengers into the nearby city centers the next day. So my group and I were forced to sleep that night. But first, like in Essipon, we had to set up our tent. We barely slept that night and could not wait for the break of day to get out.

The next day we caught the first bus to Takoradi. When we arrived in Takoradi, we made our way to Sekondi to pick up our luggage from where we had left them. Because the distances are so far apart, traveling had to start early morning. So by the time we got our luggage, found something to eat, it was late to leave for

Buduburam. That night we went to the home of a friend of ours –
Kofi – who had offered that if we were ever in Sekondi, to feel free
to stop by his place or spend the night. This was a good time to use
his offer, since we did not have anywhere to spend the night. He
was very happy to see us. We sat and talked for a while. We
informed him that we were in route to Buduburam and that we
wanted to spend the night. "No problem," he said and he quickly
prepared the room in which we were to sleep. We talked for a
while more and retired to sleep by about 12:15am. But oh, ma-ma-
ma! We could not sleep at all. The room was so hot; we were
sweating as if we were in an oven. We took off our shirts, opened
the window but none of these efforts helped our situation. The air
was still. As a matter of fact, the window opened to the exterior
wall of the home next to the house in which we were. The space
between the two houses was no more than 2.5 feet wide. How do I
know? The 3 feet window could not open wide without touching
the wall of the other house. Kofi sensed our discomfort and
informed us that if we did not mind, we could take the mattress out
of the house and sleep in the yard, under the stairs that led to the
apartment above. At first, we opposed outright to outdoors. We
had never done that before—not in Liberia, and so, of course not in
Ghana. He reassured us that we would be okay; that there was
nothing to be afraid of because there were many others who slept
out in the open every night. Most of them on mats, but we would
have a mattress. We reluctantly went outside with the mattress.
The air was blowing and it felt very good. We were still afraid;
particularly, after Kofi left us outside and went in the house. But
before long other people started gathering around where we were
and laying their mats on the ground. After a couple of minutes, we
were surrounded by many people and we felt comfortable and
secure. We fell asleep and slept well. By early morning, we were
awakened by the sound of water falling to the ground. It was a
woman taking bath in the open. It was still dark but she could be
seen. We later discovered that many people got up early in the

morning and took bath outside because many homes did not have bathroom, or the bathrooms were not hygienic enough. By the clear of day, we took the mattress inside, expressed thanks to Kofi, bade him farewell and headed straight to the parking station.

The bus was three passengers short when we arrived at the parking station. No sooner than we were seated, the last person entered the bus and we were ready to leave. It was a 44 to 55 seated coach bus. Had we come five minutes later we would have missed this bus and would have had to wait another hour or two before another bus was filled.

The ride to Buduburam, Accra, was a terrible one. The road was narrow and had many dents in it. Although paved, it felt like we were traveling on a dirt road. The four hours of a 160-mile journey took us six and the half hours, making one stop in Cape Coast, and another in Winneba. It was a relief when we finally arrived on the Buduburam Refugee Camp. I had been praying all through the journey. Despite the bad road condition, the driver was speeding uncontrollably, nearly taking every breath out of us at every curve, or a dive into a ditch. We almost ran into another car trying to dodge a hole. But thankfully, we made it at last. We were where we wanted to be—away from Sanzule, and on Buduburam, near the capital. It is not that we could not be in Sanzule, because I know Liberians can make any place livable, but we were not ready to be a part of building any new community. In fact, my reason for going to Ghana was not to stay; so I wanted to be where the work had already been done and I could rest for a while until I returned to Liberia.

BUDUBURAM, ACCRA

The Buduburam Refugee Camp is located 44 kilometers (27 miles) west of Accra, the capital of Ghana. Opened by the UNHCR in 1990, the camp was home to more than 12,000 refugees from Liberia who fled their country early in 1990 when the civil war began. It was once a populated little community but over time the place became deserted as people moved away except for a few villagers who remained in a nearby town[18]. When it became apparent that Liberians were going to be transported to Ghana as refugees, the Ghanaian authorities thought to take the Liberian refugees far away from the city. There were international NGOs, volunteer organizations and even Liberians who were providing various types of services to the refugees on the camp. The first arrivals explained that when they were taken to Buduburam, the place looked like an old deserted village. The land was bear with only a few buildings—one looking like a palace. The refugees were given tents to build and beddings (mattresses and sheets) for sleeping. There was neither electricity nor running water. But over time, Liberians transformed the deserted place into a miniature city—a place of attraction and beauty—to which many people, Ghanaians and Liberian, were gravitating. They made this refugee camp a livable place.

Arriving at the Camp, hearing the history of the place, and seeing how much Liberians had done with it, gave me a completely different impression about Liberians and their ability to be transformers of their lives and environment. The place looked like a new development—a new community. With permission, Liberians had molded dirt blocks and constructed modern, more stable homes to replace the tents they were initially given. Some of the homes were built as temporary shelters while for some, greater thought was put into their design and construction.

Primary, secondary and trade schools were constructed; so also were a modern, well-equipped clinic. Many church groups constructed large edifices. Buduburam became a full community with everything including restaurants, bars and night clubs. I was thrilled to discover that one of the clubs was named after a famous night club in Liberia, LIPS. How did they do all this as refugees? I remember many years earlier when Sudan went through their civil war, many Sudanese were taken to Liberia as refugees. But I don't remember seeing those Sudanese living fabulously like the Liberian refugees in Ghana. I am told that similar lifestyle existed among Liberians in other countries where they had gone as refugees. The more I thought about how they did it, the clearer it became to me that almost every Liberian has some relatives or contacts abroad who continue to support them, especially from the United States. Liberians abroad were sympathetic to the war situation and the suffering of their people, and were eager to help relatives and friends who were forced to flee to a foreign country. They sent money on a regular basis to help support them –$50 here and $100 there; and some, even as much as $500 at a time. It was therefore easy to understand how Liberians could live such a life as refugees. The exchange rate at the time was approximately USD$1 to ¢2050 (Ghana Cedes). It meant that having United States currency could do much for you in the Ghanaian economy. Assistance from families abroad helped Liberians in Ghana to develop the camp the way they did.

Our priority upon arriving in Buduburam was to secure a place to lay our heads when night came. Of course, our top initial search was for my mother-in-law, Ma Anna Dennis, who lived on the camp. We ran into Charles Bropleh (TCB) who had come on the camp a little earlier. He joined us, and together, we made some inquiries about Ma Anna. With the help of a young man, we located Ma Anna's place. She lived in Area G, just behind Jackson's

Night Chub. She was surprised when we walked up on her. We were both overjoyed to see one another after many years. Her eyes welled up with tears as we sat and talk—catching up on past times, touching on such basic issues including life, family, the war, situation at home, living in Ghana, future plans, etc. She explained that when they arrived, her husband took her immediately to Accra where they were with his family, but after he died, she began experiencing serious challenges from some of his family members. She lamented on how extremely difficult it was for her those days, and how she pressed through the challenges and eventually moved to the camp. Things were hard for her such that she couldn't afford to build her own house, so she rented the one in which she lived with her daughter, Sarday, and her two grand-daughters—Nayoka and Massa.

Ma Anna loves to cook—and get this right—she can really cook. Take it from a man who knows how to cook. I mean, she can cook. I think that's where her daughter, my wife, got the good cooking skills from. So, as soon as she saw us, she started to put something together for us to eat. I mean, cook some food for us. Every now and then, she would ask Sarday to put a little of this and a little of that in the pot, or she would ask her to check on the food on the fire. When the food was ready, Solo, TCB and I sat and ate like we were participating in tournament.

The house had two rooms; one in which Ma Anna slept, and the other in which Sarday and her daughters slept. It was obvious that Solo and I could not stay there, so we decided we would make connection with a few other individuals we knew were on the Buduburam Camp to spend the night until morning, when we would make other permanent arrangements for sleeping. Ma Anna insisted that I spend the night at her place. She explained that she would prepare her room for me to sleep in while she slept in the other room with Sarday and her daughters. I accepted to spend the night, but knew there and then that I would have to work with the guys to find an alternative, because it would be unfair for Ma Anna

to cram in the little bed with her daughter and granddaughters. So
the guys left to find a place they would spend the night. I walked
them a little distance away, and they agreed to meet me in the
morning. The next morning Solo and TCB joined me. We had
breakfast, and made our way around Buduburam. TCB was
stopping with some church brothers who accepted to host him
when he arrived, so inasmuch as he wanted to help us, he couldn't.
We understood. He took us to see where he was living. It was
called A47—a unique name that many people knew and could
associate the individuals with. Later in the day, we connected with
my cousin, Forti (Lynton Bropleh) who assured us he would get us
a place before the end of the day. Forti had visited me twice while
we were still at Essipon, and I had shared with him my plans to
come to Buduburam but he had made no prior arrangement.
Notwithstanding, he was confident we would be situated before the
end of the day. He took us around and gave us a great tour of the
community and helpful hints and advice about general life on
Buduburam. He really had knowledge of the community and was
well-known by many. For a moment I thought he was a local star,
but knowing his personality, I was not surprised. Forti was friendly,
helpful, jovial, and respectful and a people's person. No wonder he
was very popular. Toward the end of the day he took us to where
he lived—the home of Mr. Eric Williamson and his family. We met
and chatted with Mr. Williamson and the family who welcomed us
to Buduburam. That night we also met Ms. Jemimma Killen, a
seamstress and designer who practically lived at the Williamsons'.
Although she had a one-room house in Area C of the camp, she
never slept there. She only kept most of her clothes and other basic
necessities there. We did not hesitate to seize the opportunity to
ask permission to spend the night in her house. "You joking me?"
she asked. "I will be glad for you guys to stay there until you find a
place of your own," she added. It was a "win-win" situation for all
of us. On the one hand, it was a blessing that we could find a place
in such a short time; and on the other hand, it was a form of

security for Ms. Kellen against the threat of burglary. Indeed, coming across Ms. Kellen and a place to stay, was another manifestation of how God will create the right circumstance in your life to get you to where He wants you to be. There is no mistake in the relationships we establish and the people whose paths we cross. God always has a purpose and a plan for His children. For us, meeting Forti to take us to the Williamsons, and meeting Ms. Kellen were all orchestrations of the great God who "knows our end from our beginning." Ms. Killen gave us a key and we transferred our belongings from Ma Anna's place to our new home. We were quite satisfied and settled. We stayed at Ms. Kellen's for the duration of the time I was in Ghana – 4 months.

The pattern of our daily activities was simple for the first few days: in the morning, we had breakfast at Ma Anna's, sat with her for a while, walked around the camp, came back for dinner, and went to bed at night. Ma Anna was well-known for her good cooking. She prepared food for sale at her house. Every morning, folks stopped by to eat something before starting their day; and in the evening, they returned to have dinner and bring their day to a close. My favorite dish was banku with the okra sauce. I liked it because it reminded me much of my traditional tribal (Bassa) staple, Fufu.

The luggage we claimed from the field in Essipon was still wet from the sea water that had entered the hatch of the ship. I had not opened it since I retrieved it until coming to Buduburam. I got out my documents and laid them in the sun to dry. Then, I had Sarday rewash the clothes. Most had been damaged from the salt water, and there were not much to salvage from the suitcase. The damaged clothes were disposed of and the few good female clothes were given to Sarday. I was thankful I still had important family documents. However, I was wrong about the few shirts and pants that I thought were still good for use. One morning, as I was getting dressed, the shirt tore in the back and I had to dispose of it. Although we had purchased some clothing earlier, it was now

obvious we needed additional clothes since the once from the ship
were useless. Eventually, I had to throw away all the clothes
salvaged from the ship.

As I walked the camp and beheld what Liberians had made of it,
I realized that life is indeed about choices; what we choose to do in
the different circumstances that life puts us in—whether in
adversity, destitution or hardship, or in times of celebration and/or
merriment. It is not so much as what life hits us with that matter,
but rather, it is what we choose to do when life hits us. Liberians
had chosen to make the most of their stay as refugees beneficial and
rewarding; to change destitution into challenges for creating
dreams and spectacular success stories; to transform adversity into
opportunities. And so, the camp reflected just that. Across the camp
were training programs, skills training workshops, shops, booths
and many types of small businesses. I also saw video clubs, clothing
stores, foreign exchange booths, and cook shops. The market was
replete with foods of every kind, and just about anything
marketable that one might find in a big city market. The camp was
a classic example of what a determined people can do with their
lives and community. But what was also striking was the embrace
of "diversity" among Liberians on the camp. It was reflected in how
the people lived—in sectional groupings, like the Bassa community;
the Mano and Gio quarters; the Krahn area, and you name it, and
yet they often came together in support of activities that benefited
everyone. The skeptics might say this is a typical form of division,
but I would argue that individual people-groups have interests and
common issues that bind them, and we need to identify and respect
and encourage that. For, societies are made up of different people
groups, and the key to peaceful coexistence is the understanding,
cooperation, collaboration, partnership and respect of other
people's values, interests and concerns. The goal should be to
engage in activities that embrace the differences yet accentuate the
values and commonalities for a strong communal existence.

For example, when the first group of refugees arrived on

Buduburam, they all gathered in one place and worshiped, thanking God for his providence, and for his great mercies. The Liberian Interdenominational Assembly (LIDA) was birthed. Its purpose was to bring Liberians together in one place to worship God. I thought that was an excellent idea—whoever may have conceived it. But LIDA soon saw a vision much bigger than Liberians; it was a vision to reach beyond Liberians to Ghanaians and other parts of the world. So it changed its name to reflect that vision. The new name became Christian Interdenominational Assembly (CRIDA). CRIDA grew over the years, and with concerted effort and support, a modern edifice was constructed. However, as times went by, the leadership of various denominations decided to reach out to their members and to support their living as refugees. They wanted to bring various types of services to all Liberians, but preferred to channel everything through a smaller and manageable group. To do so, members of these denominations were encouraged to establish worship centers, and to institute the denomination's structure of leadership through whom intended services would be administered and/or controlled. They were also concerned about continuing the doctrine of individual doctrinal engagement with traditional ways of worship. Hence, churches of all denominations were established—Methodist, Baptist, Assembly of God, Episcopal, Adventist and Catholics, as well as many newly established independent churches. As a result, several services were brought to Buduburam for the benefit of all Liberians.

Let's take, for example, that there was one leadership for all Liberians on Buduburam. It would mean that services and projects would have to be introduced or implemented one at a time to ensure efficiency and accountability and control. This would have been an ineffective process for catering to the volume of and diverse needs of Liberians. But because of the various denominational groups, for example, many services and/or projects were implemented simultaneously, thereby giving a wider range of options to Liberians and serving many needs at the same time. Let it be known that not only Christians were providing social and other types of services to Liberians, but also other religious groups such as Muslims, Hindus, and the Bahias as well. Eventually, Buduburam became flooded with churches and mosques and other types of worship centers, but the benefits were noticeable and enormous: The Lutheran Church built one clinic; the Catholic Church built a second clinic; the United Methodist Church established a school, while the Bong County citizens constructed the Library. In addition, the United Methodist Church, in partnership with the All Saints Pentecostal Church, constructed several toilets around the camp. The UMC also ran a Woodwork/Carpentry Shop, a Computer Literacy Program, a Substance Abuse Program, and a Skills Training Program for single women and young mothers who had no domestic skill. Other skill-building programs included tie and dye and batik, baking, sewing and woodwork. Very skillful, trained and experienced Liberians like Eroy Smith, Charles Bonar and others, oversaw these programs - intended to help make the refugees self-sufficient and self-sustaining. These are just a few of the different services and opportunities that embracing diversity brought to the Liberian people living on the Buduburam Refugee Camp. In my mind, Buduburam presented a perfect opportunity—away from home—for Liberians to learn to appreciate the value of diversity and develop a form of togetherness that could impact national unity, peace and reconciliation at home.

Unfortunately, not all the residents on Buduburam and targeted beneficiaries took advantage of those opportunities. Many days, as I walked around the camp, I saw young men and women, and children, who could have been in school, roaming the camp doing nothing. It was disheartening to see the vast amount of wasted time in the midst of help and opportunities. Could it be that some of these young people did not have proper adult guidance? Or could it be that these young people were overwhelmed with the thought of living on their own, having the freedom they once dreamed of, to dictate their own course of action? I am not sure, but I do know that there were many young people living on the camp by themselves, living in groups of five or more, with no parental or adult guidance. The peer pressure was high and influential in a negative way, especially if one or two of a young person's associates were not interested in education. What they did instead was get dressed and go to town, being the fashionable divas of the camp and having fun. As a result, many young girls ended up sleeping with men for whatever financial or other assistance they could get. I don't want to say, but it was a form of teen prostitutes. As for the young men, most were involved in doing odd jobs around the camp for money. It was a difficult situation for any young person to be in. Because of the lack of structure at home, curiosity and the need to fit-in, to conform, many young people had fallen prey to the peer pressure. Some dropped out of school while others declined significantly in their school activities.

One day, I encountered two young men arguing and about to get into a fist fight. I was able to break it up and spoke of other ways they could use their time. When the argument was over and we had the time to chat, I asked them about school and how they were doing. Both informed me that they had dropped out of school because no one could help them. I found it hard to believe because most of the programs on the camp at the time were sponsored through grant or some assistance and no fees were being charged. Later, they confessed that they are looking for money and had no time for school. I wondered how many other young people thought or felt that way. I pitched in some of my youth development motivational lines and even asked if they would continue school if I paid for them to go. Their response shocked me even mote. "Papay, this is war time, nobody going to school in Liberia." What they meant was as long as there was war in Liberia, there was no need to go to school. What they did not realize is that they were not in Liberia, and that the war would not last forever.

"What will your life look like or what will your life be after 5, 10 or 15 years from now when the war is over?" "What would you do?" "How do you intend to support yourself or your family if you get one?" I asked. We talked for hours—there was nothing to do anyway. But I felt excited that I succeeded in getting through to them on seizing the opportunity to develop themselves for their own good and nobody's. I asked them to think about it and what they wanted to do, and planned to meet the next morning at Ma Anna's place for breakfast. We met the next day as planned, had breakfast and sat and talked for some more. "Have you thought about anything you would like to do to better yourselves?" I asked finally. They explained that they would like to take up some basic skills training but were not interested in regular school. I understood, because they were much older for specific age-appropriate classes and felt they would be ridiculed. To conclude the story: I discussed the possibility with Mr. Charles Bonar who ran a woodwork shop and they were enrolled. I checked on their progress during my stay in Buduburam and it was encouraging. Charles was impressed with their commitment to learn and the devotion they brought to the trade. Oh, how I wished I could have helped more young people, but I couldn't. "How many young people are out there who have been missed?" I kept asking this question over and over to myself. This is where I thought that some of the organizations failed. Perhaps, a program that identified this category of young people and served in guidance / counseling roles on issues that encouraged education, moral integrity or self-development would have been helpful in getting some, if not all of these young people, off the streets. As a result, there was a rise in child labor and teenage pregnancy among the youth population. It baffled me for a while—seeing the laid-back and don't-care attitude in the youth and some of the adults alike. One would think that fleeing a war situation, people would be more concerned about developing themselves through formal education, trade or other means, especially with the opportunity to do so, knowing that that opportunity was non-existent at home. Instead, many people acted as if they were on a long vacation—enjoying and enjoying and enjoying—with no end in view.

A marked contrast however, was glaring among young people who lived with their parents or were under the guidance of an adult. They were the ones in school, in the skills training programs, and engaged in other activities of self-development. To their advantage, they did not have to find food for themselves, or buy their own clothes, or pay rent if it had to be paid. Their parents were there to provide basic necessities, and all they had to do was be children and go to school, which they did.

It is no secret that the war scattered Liberians in many different places around the country and abroad; many others lost their lives as we well know. And still for others, we just didn't know where they were. In many instances, when people were not seen for a while in Liberia, and there was no information as to where they had traveled to, it was automatically assumed that they were dead—especially if close relatives, friends or neighbors couldn't be certain if they traveled or not. So, many people came "alive from the dead" in Ghana—people who were presumed dead just popped out at once. It was an exhilarating feeling to know that some people were still alive after words had spread about their death. I met some very good old school friends and community and church acquaintances who, in Liberia, were presumed dead. Come to think about it, Buduburam was like the place to be. Almost everyone that was missed in Monrovia was there; it was like a grand reunion point. I saw Paul Glaydor, a church brother of mine; I saw my cousin Leon Nagbe; I saw Bunchie Bright, a friend from high school; I saw Tanyonnoh, a friend of a friend; I saw Patricia Jallah, a childhood friend; and Oretha Weeks, a church sister; I saw Nkadi Obiamiwe, also from my church. Everywhere I passed, I came upon a friend, an acquaintance or a familiar face from Monrovia.

For those who don't know much about Liberia, it is such a small country that it seems like everybody knows everybody. If you lived

in Monrovia or its environs, someway-somehow, you crossed path
with people. You may not know them personally or may have
never spoken to them in your life, but you had seen them many
times on many different occasions. They were not your friends; you
just knew them because we all went to just about the same places,
or crossed path at usual and unusual places—in the community, at
school or work, the clubs, basketball courts, football games,
parades, weddings, funerals, parties, standing at the bus stops,
trying to get a taxi cab, in the market, at the cinema, etc. Each day,
I ran into someone new. Everyone seemed happy, well-groomed
and looked healthy. These people didn't have the typical refugee
look—sad, unkempt or poverty-stricken. To many, it was like being
on an extended vacation—relaxed, no pressure for work, too much
play, fun and pleasure. Some of the young women dressed each day
like they were going to a fashion show—I mean, immaculate and
gorgeous.

I couldn't imagine the level of good time going on in
Buduburam. It was as if nothing was happening in Liberia. People
appeared to have arrived; they were complacent and satisfied with
life as it was. But who would not? They did not have to work for
the stipend and/or monthly contributions they received from
relatives and friends abroad. With that, they could afford to live the
lavage, loose life-style—eat, drink and be merry. The more I
thought about it, the more the realization hit me: most or some of
these people had not had the direct experience of the war; they did
not see the houses burnt, nor did they see or hear the shootings in
the streets. They did not walk through check points, or had to be
told to roll in muddy waters; they did not eat" five fingers" or
"palm cabbage"; they did not walk several miles looking for food,
or sleep in houses with no doors; they didn't see or hear the little
boys soldiers insult the elders, nor did they see little girls shoot
pregnant women. They did not see people taken from a line and
shot in front of others, nor did they see a child soldier rape a
relative in their presence. There were many things about Liberia

and the war that many folks on Buduburam had no idea about, except for what they heard on the news. You ask me how I know. Many of these people left the country just when the war started. So, in a sense the way they lived compared to someone like me who had lived throughout every warring condition and dynamic was understandable. This was sufficient reason for me not to be hard on them for their lifestyle of some sort of opulence. Notwithstanding, I expected them to be empathetic about the situation at home, knowing the threat from which they had fled and the raging devastation and destruction of lives and property that were no secret to the world. It was their people who were dying and their country that was being torn apart.

The City of Accra was less than an hour from Buduburam. On my first trip there one early Wednesday morning, we went to the area called "Kwame Nkrumah Circle"—an area I had read about in African History, but now had an opportunity to see firsthand. It was a great feeling just walking around Circle and seeing parts of the city. Of course, you could not miss the stature of one of Ghana's famous presidents, Kwame Nkrumah, after whom the area is named. I had not seen this type of intercession arrangement until that time. It looked complex yet simple at the same time. Standing there watching the cars make their turns in the circle was spectacular. We walked through the market area, went to neighboring local communities and ended up in one of the many chop bars along the streets. There we ate some fufu and palm soup. Thereafter, we made several trips to the city. Some of the places we visited included the Tema Port, Osu, the E. K. Kotoka Airport, the Liberian Embassy, the big market areas, etc.

I will never forget one of the fun-filled trips we made to the city. It was to watch an international soccer match between Liberia (Lone Star) and the Gambia (Scorpions) on July 44, 1996. The game was part of the African Cup of Nations series, and was originally slated to be played in Liberia. But because of the war, the fragile political and security situation, the match was transferred to Ghana.

It was one of the highlights of Liberian refugees living in Ghana—to see and cheer their national team, amidst the trouble at home. A local organization called Serving All Liberians Everywhere (SALE) was instrumental in mobilizing support for the Lone Star. Mr. Eric Williamson, Director of **SALE**, organized and was guest on a number of local radio and television stations, promoting the "Liberian Pride." He called on all Liberians living in Ghana and friends of Liberia to turn out in mass numbers to show support for the Lone Star. I remember listening to one of his interviews on the radio when he said, ".... No matter who you are, if you're coming to the game, be sure you wear red or white or blue, or any combination of the three colors." The stadium reflected a positive response to this appeal. Not only did **SALE** mobilize for the game but it also organized transportation to get individuals from the camp to the stadium and back. Liberians showed up in mass to cheer some of their favorite football stars including Kevin Segbe, James Salinsa Debbah, and of course, George "Oppong" Weah. The momentum was so very high and the publicity so widespread that even Ghanaians who went on the field that day, wore the Liberian national colors—red, white and blue. The Lone Star brought great pride to all Liberians at home and abroad when they won the game 4–1. The players must have felt at home and equally proud of the level of support and cheers from Liberians and friends in Ghana. We boosted their morale and courage, and they played their best.

The Ghanaians are a nationalistic people and profound soccer lovers too. But seeing them dressed in red, white and blue spoke much to the level of mobilization that **SALE** did for the game. What was even inconceivable was the fact that Ghanaians, much more than Liberians, wanted to see "George Oppong Weah." At the time, he was the holder of two prestigious: "FIFA World Player of the Year" and "The African Footballer of the Year." They wanted to see him play in person, because he was regarded as one of the greatest African players of all time and of his generation—a true pride of Africa. Therefore, they came en mass, and wore the colors of the Lone Star—to identify with the world's best player. There is a joke in Liberia that the Ghanaians love themselves so much that they often associate all good things with Ghana. If it is good, it's got to be Ghanaian. We even heard someone mention that George Oppong Weah must have some Ghanaian background or lineage. He said, "It must be that George Weah's father's father's father must have been a Ghanaian. Even his name 'Oppong,' is Ghanaian." I think many Ghanaians believed that. No wonder the entire field was filled with spectators in the Lone Star colors.

That evening, back on the camp, celebration took place everywhere. From the video clubs to the nightclubs, and in homes, people were jubilating. It was like celebrating Christmas—people drinking and dancing, music blaring virtually throughout the camp. Ghanaians were celebrating as if their country had won the match. Liberians were united in support of the Lone Star, and the team did not disappoint us. What we witnessed on that day was the power of sports as a reconciling tool. Yes, it has that much of a power to bring people together. It always has; throughout the years prior to the war and during the war, it has generated the single most event that has always brought ALL Liberians together. The Lone Star lives forever.

Although I did not plan to stay in Ghana long, I still felt that while I was there, it was important that I engaged in some form of educational activity until such time when I was ready to return home. Both Solo and I had discussed that Bible College or Seminary would be an appropriate choice. I think this decision was driven by the experiences we have had, and how God moved through the many difficult periods of our journey and brought us through situations we never thought we would have easily gotten through. Moreover, we had been studying the Word and praying and delving deeper and deeper into the Bible that we felt the need to back our understanding with actual theological training. I had also felt a call to ministry many years earlier, and had struggled with what specifically I was called to do. Somehow, I felt I was called to teaching ministry; whereas Solo felt a call to preaching ministry. We inquired about Bible colleges and seminaries within Accra and decided to enroll at the Ghana Christian College and Seminary. Preliminary discussions were held with authorities at the college and the process and requirements were given to us. First, we had to sit an entrance examination. Both of us passed the entrance and were admitted.

Exactly two weeks after we commenced school, I received word that things had subsided and that our office—the Liberian Bank for Development and Investment (LBDI)—had re-opened and staffs were requested to return home. Another workmate of mine, Gartoun George, had also travelled on *Bulk Challenge* and was now on the Buduburam as well. He informed me that he had received word for us to return to work. I checked and confirmed the information and made arrangements to leave.

JOURNEY BACK HOME

Buduburam was an interesting place. I had been on the camp for just a little over three months, but because too much was going on in Ghana, the short time I stayed seemed like years. I made some new friends and acquaintances; I participated in community activities like workshops and musical concerts; I was involved in the church and provided basic assistance to young people in the form of counseling. But it was time to leave; it was time to end my forced extended vacation, if I should give it a title. It was time to return to the love of my life—my wife and children. Indeed, it was time to get back to things that kept me busy—family, work, church and community activities.

Since I could not take back the clothes that were damaged from the sea water, I decided to purchase some clothes for my wife and children. Ghana had some very good clothes for cheap prices. Their African clothes are among the best designs in the region. I spent a few days getting things for my family, and when my shopping was done, I packed by suitcase and was ready for the return journey. Since planes were still not landing in Liberia, the only other option I had was to travel by land. With the experience of *Bulk Challenge* fresh in my mind, I sure was not contemplating traveling by ship. So, I checked out the information for the next available bus to Liberia. Because of Liberians on the Buduburam Camp, travel to Liberia by road had become very frequent with Liberians going back and forth. Although there were several busses that traveled between Liberia and Ghana, I was advised to travel with a certain driver. I checked for him around the camp for a few days and located him one Friday evening after he had come from Liberia. We chatted briefly about my plan to travel with him. Together, we agreed to leave on September 13th, 1996.

When the day came, I said good bye to my buddy and friend, Solomon, and my mother-in-law and her family. In the days before, I informed most of my acquaintances of my anticipated trip back home. Some were trying to persuade me to stay. But I had even more compelling reasons to return that their attempts proved futile. As excited as I was, the trip was not an excitement at all. Extortion from immigration personnel was a sickening experience, especially driving through Côte d' Ivoire (The Ivory Coast). The officials would speak French and leave it up to you to interpret what they said and respond accordingly. They would ask for a certain amount for no reason. It had nothing to do with violations of any kind, and if you didn't make it available, they held on to your travel document until you paid. As a result, the trip was long and dreary.

At one particular check point, we were held for nearly two hours. An officer had called us into the makeshift office on the side of the road. Inside the tent, he took our traveling documents and requested that each passenger paid CFA 1,500 of the Ivorian money before passing through. I observed that only non-Ivorians were being asked to pay these outrageous fees. When the Ivorians stepped into the tent and spoke French or the indigenous language, they were allowed to go back into the bus and wait. Some of us foreigners who had and could afford, paid, retrieved our documents and got back on the bus. There were some passengers who could not afford to pay any money, simply because they did not anticipate the extortion, and more so, because they did not have any additional money. The Ivorian passengers began complaining and fussing with the officers. Some of them threatened to report the corrupt behavior. When it became apparent that they could not get money out of those passengers, they returned their traveling documents and we continued the journey. I was hoping we did not encounter any such check points again, but there were few others, although not as difficult as the one mentioned.

I was glad when we arrived in Danane—a town in western Côte d'Ivoire near the Guinean and Liberian borders. It became the destination for most Liberian refugees fleeing the conflict across the border. As such, the population in that little boarder town increased exponentially. There were almost as many Liberians as were Ivoirians living in Danane. I felt at home and was relieved from the torment of the road journey. I met many Liberians—a few I knew before. So I stayed a full day in Danane and rested to continue the journey to Monrovia. The next day, I crossed over to the Liberian side into Butuo—a once prosperous cocoa-growing border town in Liberia. At least we were on home soil, familiar grounds and I knew that the rest of the journey from there on to my final destination would be much smoother. Not so true, I discovered. We also encountered the Liberian share of extortion, although the officers were not as demanding and unreasonable as their counterparts in the Ivory Coast. At many of the checkpoints, we smooth-talked our way through or left it up to the driver of the vehicle to "shake-hands" with the officers at the posts.

We stopped in Ganta to ease ourselves and to find something to eat. We went into a "Cook Shop" (a local restaurant) where I purchased a bowl of "ghengba" (a Liberian dish) made from cassava, and swallowed down with a special kind of slimy sauce. I drank a bottle of Coca Cola (Coke for short) and was ready for the rest of the way home. It was my first real meal since I left the Ivory Coast. I purchased some dried snails from the petty traders to take home with me. We also made a stop in Gbarnga, where I purchased some dried meat. It was a fun-filled last leg of the journey. Eventually, we made it through from the boarder all the way to Paynesville Red Light— (the parking station), and then from there to my home in the ELWA community where my family had returned after being in the port area for about a month and a half.

I was overjoyed to be reunited with my family. My wife and children looked healthy and were even happier to see me. I can understand the absence of a dad in a home can mean much, just as the presence means a million. I began to feel bad that I had left them for so long. Notwithstanding, the more I thought and felt that sad, the more I realized that there was nothing I could have done to avoid the situation. What will be will be; and I have resigned to accepting the things I cannot change and allowing God to work out the difference in ways that bring the most benefit to me—regardless.

My mother and father were at my home when I arrived. A few of my siblings joined us later. My wife prepared some food as if for a party. Well, we can say it was a welcome home party after all. We had prayer and ate and had a wonderful reunion. It was good to be home. The trip was worth the experience and time. Many memorable moments have stuck with me and have helped shift my perception of life. I will cherish them forever.

MEMORABLE MOMENTS & LESSONS LEARNED

My entire journey on the *Bulk Challenge* and in Ghana was a worthy experience. I cannot discount anything. There were good times and bad times, funny instances and foolish moments, sometimes emanating from weird behavior, but I have chosen to write this section to highlight some of the most memorable moments and the lessons learned from them. I hope readers will find this as entertaining as much as educational.

Uninvited Guests at a Wedding

It has been said that there is a second person – a "second you" – an identical resemblance to every individual that walks the earth. How true this may be for every individual, I do not know. But what I do know is that I have seen people who look very much alike although they are not related. People from different parts of the world have very close resemblance and can pass as twins. A resemblance, according to dictionary definition, "... is a similarity in appearance." Children usually have a strong *resemblance* to their biological parents. Relatives often have resemblances because they share the same genes. But strange enough, those who are not related sometimes do resemble and that is one of the intriguing things in nature. Perhaps you, the reader, may have a resemblance to a famous person.

Sometimes you come across a person and he or she looks exactly like someone you know so very well; but your attempt to get their attention and/or make contact proves futile because that person is not who you think he/she is. Therefore, he/she does not pay you any mind as you seek to attract the appropriate attention. The person has a different name than the one you called. For example, a person born in Alabama has close resemblance to a person born in Africa or Canada, but actually, with no family connection or blood relationship. They just look alike.

One day Solo and I were walking around the Buduburam community and we saw people dressed up for a wedding ceremony, apparently coming from the church ceremony and going for the reception. It must have been special and well planned, with lots of money spent on the preparation. The reception was being held in one of the largest reception pavilions on the camp. It was nicely decorated. The guests were assembling when we walked by. Although we were not in suits and ties, we were appropriately dressed, and could blend very well with the attendees. We decided that since we did not have anything particular to do that warm Saturday afternoon, we would "crush" the wedding. After all, we were all Liberians. We inched our way into the reception. Initially, we stood toward the back of the hut near the entrance. Interestingly, as guests entered the place, they would turn to Solo to speak to him and shake his hand. Over and over, people walked up to him to shake his hand. He couldn't get over it; they would walk past me but stop to speak to him and with a smile too. "But what's going on brother-man," he asked. I just laughed, and then said further: "Brother-man, you are the man!" What confused us was the fact that we had been on the camp less than three weeks, and barely knew people, except a few but certainly, not any of these people coming to the reception. They were as strange as a cat having horns. Then, we finally understood why. A glance at one of the wedding programs said it all. The groom and Solomon had stark resemblance. They could pass as twins. The guests were speaking to Solo because they thought he was the brother of the groom. We looked at the name on the program sheet. The whole scenario was strange. We did not know this groom at all. Well, since no one asked us, we did not have to say a word. A good rule: "no ask no tell." We decided to "go with the flow" as long as it benefited us at the moment. We stood at the entrance as folks greeted us and passed by. Then suddenly, someone asked, "Are you guys not going to sit?" It was an elderly man. So, we walked in with him and his friend and sat at the same table. "What have we to lose?" we thought. We didn't know many people, and certainly the people didn't know us, for we were new comers to the camp. The table was up front, just few tables down from the bridal party's table. It looked like one of those tables that were reserved for family members, although it had no label. We sat before we realized that, and were ashamed to get out and leave. We engaged the men at the table in conversation and told few stories to pass the time. We laughed and talked and had a good time talking. They appeared to be family members of the bride who were just pleased to be sitting with the brother of the groom – or so they thought. Then the bridal party arrived and "boom" we saw it all. Yes, indeed, the groom and Solo looked strikingly alike. More significantly, the groom was from a tribe totally different from ours. We heard a Liberian language that was not ours.

The reception ceremony began with the usual remarks and toast to the newly wedded couple. They were elegantly dressed in African attire; bride and groom in white "Bazzam" with gold design, while the bridal party had light gray three piece designed "Bazzam" outfits. The food was served, and I must confess, it was good. Our table was well served, and we ate sumptuously. It was funny because every time I looked up, I saw the groom looking in our direction. Solo was making sure not to make any eye contact with the guy. He did not even stir in the direction of the honorees' table. Most, if not all of the people thought, Solo was a family member, except the Bride and the Groom. From where we sat, we couldn't hear what was being said, but we sensed that they were discussing our presence. Both the bride and groom were looking in our direction and murmuring in their seats. I reasoned their conversation may have gone something like this:

BRIDE – "Is that your brother over there?"

GROOM – "No, I don't know that guy from anywhere."

BRIDE – "But who is he and what is he doing at the family table?"

GROOM – "I don't know; I thought he was your family or some sort."

BRIDE – "How will he be my family, and the man looks just like you? Are you sure he's not one of your cousins or some family member?"

GROOM – "I told you, I don't know the man. I've never seen him before. This is my first time seeing him, and yes he looks like one of my brothers, but I know for sure none of them is here."

We were beginning to feel uneasy and so we decided to leave the reception earlier. The day was well spent. We had eaten and were filled, and we didn't even know the people. It worked well for us, and we left.

After the wedding, we learned the whole story about the wedding and the groom. He had come from the United States to get married to his fiancé he had left in Ghana a few years earlier. He knew some people and had friends in Ghana but no family was with him at the time. This was one of the memorable moments of our stay in Ghana. We saw an opportunity to eat some good food after a long day and we took advantage of the phenomenon called resemblance. Did I say "opportunity"? Yes! As odd as it may sound, there is a lesson we can learn about opportunity in this situation. The *Oxford Dictionary* defines "Opportunity" as "A set of circumstances that makes it possible to do something." Prince Nico, a renowned African musician, once said in his hit song "Sweet Mother": "opportunity comes but once in this world." What he meant is that not often does an opportunity reappears   and since we cannot predict infrequent reoccurrences, it is best we make the most of it while we have it; for we may never get another chance at it. Notwithstanding, we understand and believe that opportunities do come in many different forms and fashions—sometimes only once, sometimes seldom repeated, and sometimes never ever resurfaced. So, whether it has to do with empowerment, work, relationship, service, or helping others, people should do what they can with it, with all possible might and with an attitude of urgency to get the best possible outcome.

The measure of our fortitude and ability to advance in life is not contained in how many opportunities come our way, but what we do with each opportunity to change our circumstances and transform our lives and the lives of others around us. It is about turning challenges into courage; barriers to bridges; confusion into cooperation; and problems into possibilities. When we can see beyond the difficulties and constraints of life, into the possibilities and options in every situation—good or bad—then we are fueling our energy-drives that will propel us to overcome obstacles.

Tommy Sharrow is a coworker of mine. I have known him for many years — "from back in the days"— folks would say. We were members of the same church in Liberia – the S. Trowen Nagbe United Methodist Church – where we served together in the Men's Fellowship. In a discussion with him one cold January morning, he said, "Life does not stop where the struggle begins." Initially, I found it difficult comprehending what he meant, but as we spoke I caught the bigger picture of what he was actually saying: Life does not end because you find yourself in the struggles of life; that even in the worst of times, we should never give up hopes but keep our spirits alive, always believing that a better day is coming. I thought what Tommy said was profound; because, indeed, there is an opportunity in every situation that requires us to do something. Some situation might offer the opportunity to be honest, truthful or sincere; while other situations might call for a demonstration of maturity. Some might present an opportunity to show acts of kindness, while others might be an opportunity to fight for your rights. Positive living calls each of us to find an opportunity to move forward in every situation—even the negative situations—that tends to break our spirits and crush our dreams. I came across this quote from an anonymous author on Facebook: "Life is like a camera... focus on what's important, capture what is good, develop from the negatives, and if things don't work out, take another shot.[19]" This quote, I believe, summarized Tommy's observation on that January morning.

Today, as I reminisce about that day when Solo and I crushed that wedding, we wished we had not placed ourselves in that situation. It could have been very embarrassing had someone acted to engage us that day. We've laughed about it now because the embarrassment never happened. It is funny how with confidence, we sat through that wedding reception, but we also acknowledge it was a wrong move. Notwithstanding, it is one of those things that make up the total experiences of a person's life.

Riding on the Bus

Ghanaians are known for their nationalism. Unlike Liberians who have several tribes or local languages and no national language, except English. All Ghanaians learn and speak "Twi" in addition to their individual tribal languages. Because of this, Ghanaians can accomplish a great deal together. In addition to Twi, some Ghanaians also speak Gan along with other major African languages. However, one observation I made about Ghanaians, for the time I lived among them, is that as long as you were speaking a language, you were considered a Ghanaian regardless of where you came from. This was funny because Ghanaians, unlike Liberians, cannot differentiate among the various Ghanaian languages. Perhaps, because the country has many tribes and many of them are unfamiliar with the other tribes, or have never heard them spoken before. Liberians, on the other hand, can easily determine from where a person came by the language they speak. Maybe because there are only 16 tribes in Liberia compared to Ghana. But in addition to our ability to detect Liberian tribal languages, we have a sixth sense that can clearly discern different groups from around Africa and sometimes, other parts of the world. For Ghanaians, this is a difficult task. So, whenever they heard a language that was unfamiliar or they didn't understand, their first assumption was that it is one of the Ghanaian tribes from another region.

Moving around Ghana was becoming a problem for most Liberians because some Liberians had begun engaging in criminal and other antisocial activities that upset Ghanaians to the point where they were beginning to mistreat, ill-treat or become indifferent toward Liberians they encountered. Whether on the bus or in the market place, Liberians were spoken to in harsh, cruel and unpleasant ways. One of the things we observed was that whenever we spoke English, it was easily determined to be "Liberian English." Our accent is not as strong as those of the Ghanaians or Nigerians. As a result, Ghanaians would not speak to us on the bus, or even shift or move aside to allow us sit beside them. They would make cruel statements like "You Liberians should make haste and park your things and leave our country." Or, "You Liberians are thieves." For us who were just arriving on the camp, it was embarrassing to hear that some Liberians had misbehaved in Ghana, and now we were bearing the cost. It was like the old saying: "One bad apple spoils the whole bunch." In any case, it was unfair to cast a collective guilt on all Liberians, but, equally so, it was understandable why many, many Ghanaians behaved the way they did.

Howbeit, we had to find a way to get around Ghana without being noticed as Liberians and treated awfully. Don't get me wrong; it was not so bad that Liberians could not travel in Ghana. We just didn't want to be bothered with the stirs and side comments when we traveled, especially in commuter buses. We wanted to have conversation without all the attention. Yet, it was difficult to disguise ourselves totally. The way we dress is Liberian outright, different from how Ghanaians dress. Our hairstyles are different; most Ghanaian men love to keep bushy hair, while their women wear low haircuts. In Ghana, it was easy to spot a Liberian. Sometimes, Ghanaians' gaze spoke volumes as to their sensitivity toward us. Eventually, Solo and I agreed to speak our native language (Bassa) whenever we were out and about.

One day, while traveling within Accra, we entered a bus and someone from the back shouted, "Liberia-fo!" Now generally "fo" in Twi means "person" or "one," as in Osagyefo, meaning one who saves. Yet in the context of engaging with Liberians, the word seemed to have a disapproving edge to it. It seemed to suggest disrespect. When one of them engaged us, speaking Twi to us, Solomon began speaking Bassa to him. We couldn't understand them; they couldn't understand us. Then we began having our conversation in Bassa, and they all became quiet, apparently assuming that we were from another region of the country.

Initially, we did not know what reaction it would spark but it worked to our advantage and saved us the unnecessary embarrassment of being treated differently or answering questions we often faced from anti-Liberians. Eventually, it worked for us that one time, and did all the time we were out riding on the bus, or walking the streets, or in the marketplace. We spoke Bassa. We traveled freely thereafter, enjoying the fun of responding to them in Bassa when they spoke to us in whatever Ghanaian language. Sometimes we even cursed them in Bassa, and since they didn't understand, we were just satisfied to be cursing.

The lesson to be learned from this experience is simple. Be careful how you make generalizations so that they do not become stereotypes. Do not make generalizations on the basis of a few isolated incidents or situations. Since all people are different, you should never assume an individual is exactly like others; however, a generalization can possibly give insight to the tendencies of a particular group of people. It helps us understand and make sense of our world and situations around us. It is when we overgeneralize and use such generalizations to negatively refer to people, that we easily gravitate to the realm of stereotypes which can be harmful. Besides, stereotypes often leave no room for exceptions, resulting to situations where the just suffer with the unjust. Such situations do not allow for other characteristics of individuals to be seen or appreciated. We eventually miss the impact generalizations may have on interpersonal relationships.

Shocking Pulpit Outrage

Another memorable event occurred at church. The day after we arrived on the campus in Essipon, several pastors and church officials from Sekondi and Takoradi came to welcome us, the refugees. Some of them brought food, water and clothes; others came to share words of comfort, hope and assurance. They were all empathetic about our situation and extended invitations to visit and worship with them, and offered that if there was any particular help we needed, we could ask without hesitation. One particular pastor, and I will not say what his name is, spent much of that night with us. We talked about the trip and many other issues, as well as our personal situations. He was young and friendly and seemed genuinely interested in helping refugees and building relationships with us. He was also very well read in African history and knew a lot about Liberia—not just the war, but some of the nation's heyday role in international politics. We connected with Pastor John in many ways and decided to visit his church. It turned out that we loved the church service and worship experience, and thought to make it our place of worship as long as we were in that region of the world. Over time, we invited some of the younger men and women to accompany us to church. A few of them with musical skills joined the choir. One of the young men could play the piano. It was a small but outstanding choir. If you know anything about Ghanaians, one thing is for sure: they love to sing and can sing very well like most Africans. They play different types of musical instruments too. We were at church early each time to participate and enjoy the full anointing from the praise and worship team. We never missed that. It was the best part of the service. Someone said, "There are generally three ministries taking place in every worship service: the ministries of prayer, music, and of the proclamation of the Word." One, if not all, must speak to a worshiper, and for me it is the music. I got so much inspiration, courage and uplifting feelings from the singing. That time meant much to me and helped my faith growth.

One Sunday morning as the pastor preached and attempted to warn the young ladies of the church, I heard these words distinctively: "You have to be mindful of those 'F***king' Liberian boys." It was a total shock to us, hearing those words spoken by a pastor and up from the pulpit. "It must have been something very bad that the boys had done," I thought to myself. I pinched Solo sitting next to me and he acknowledged the outburst of the pastor. After church, we decided to look into what had happened and speak to the young men so that no behavior of them would be interpreted negatively against all Liberians. We spoke with the music director and asked if anything had gone wrong on the night before, anything involving the Liberian boys. He said nothing to his knowledge and asked why we were concerned. We promised to get back with him once we got some information. So we caught up with the boys and they explained that after rehearsal that Saturday night, they were talking with some of the girls at the back of the church and one of the boys pulled a girl very close that she was standing between his legs. When the pastor came out of the building and saw the group of them and the position in which they were, he was not pleased with the attitude of the boys but he was equally disappointed with that of the girls. So he asked the girls to go home in preparation for service, and cautioned the boys to be careful as they traveled back to the camp. They expressed shock over the pastor's outrage from the pulpit.

We later shared that information with the music director and explained that the language which the pastor used from the pulpit was indication that he was mad about something. We said he had cursed. "What cursing?" the director asked. "He used the 'F-word'" I responded. "Do you remember pastor saying those 'F***king Liberian boys'?" I asked. He laughed about it, and for a moment I almost lost it. Why was he laughing at the pastor cursing at my fellow Liberians? And then he said, "Oh is that what you are talking about? That is no cursing at all. Pastor only meant 'foolish' when he said 'f***king, that's all. He was not mad and that is not a curse word to us." The explanation shocked us even more. From whence we came, the "F-word" used in any form is vulgar and considered a curse word, unacceptable and socially offensive. And, worse of all, using it on the pulpit was incomprehensible, but we had to respect other people's culture and way of life. That is the essence of diversity, and the value of traveling to another country other than your own. We asked a few other people in that region, and got the same response—that he only meant "foolish."

That night, on the camp, we gathered the boys and explained to them what the pastor meant and how what he had said did not mean what it sounded like or what we know it to be. We further advised them to be mindful of their interactions with the females, noting that the environment was religious and as strangers in the area, we didn't want to be perceived negatively. We agreed that there was nothing wrong with making new friends, but encouraged them to take time to study the people so as not to take wrong steps and offend anyone. Our young people were thankful for our advice and confessed that they were contemplating not going back to the church, but they thought to reconsider that decision. That night, as I lay in bed, I replayed the pastor's outburst and the situation leading to that outburst and reflected on my own youthful days. I smiled and thought, "Perhaps, we would have done worse" because we were risky kids growing up.

The lesson to be learned here is to take time to understand

other people and their ways of life—speech, mannerism, sociability, etc. so as not to rush to judgment based on a statement or an action. For too often we use our own values to judge the behaviors and attitudes of others; but as the world becomes more global, it is important that we learn to understand, recognize, embrace and appreciate the diversities of the various people with whom we interact. We must all have open minds and willing spirit to see beyond our individual value systems.

Getting Direction

There were many interesting experiences we had in Ghana. One of the great lessons we learned earlier during our stay was to detect when someone was being insincere and/or untruthful. It took two or three occasions to bring us to this realization, especially after this event I am about to share.

It was a hot sunny afternoon when Solo and I encountered this no-use, good-for-nothing Ghanaian who did not know the very city in which he was born and had grown up in. We were looking for a particular building; I am not sure why, but it was important that we found the building. We thought we were close by and decided to ask a gentleman who looked like someone who knew the area very well. Of course our assumption was wrong; he was one of the guys who would not say "I don't know." When we asked him how to get to the building, his response was this: "Okay... if you take this road, you go walk 'par...' there is a certain chop bar; you will make a right and as you make the right, there is a 'this thing' and the 'prace' is just there. You can't miss it." Although we were unclear about this direction, he said it with such a conviction that we proceeded immediately to follow what he had said. Now, let me clarify the language our friend used in showing us the way: 1) "par" – means you will walk a little distance; 2) "chop bar" is a little booth in which food and other marketable items are sold along the side of the streets. It looks like a typical newsstand in the Western world, or lotto booth in Liberia; 3) "this thing" – is what Ghanaians say for anything they cannot readily remember by specific name. For example, if they were referring to a car and couldn't remember the word "car" they would say "this thing," pointing to the car; or speaking of money, you might hear someone say "you have to give me my 'this thing'"— "this thing" meaning, "money." Therefore, "this thing" is a substitute word for anything. When the direction to the building was being given, we didn't know what "this thing" meant. Lastly, the fellow used "prace," which is how most Ghanaians pronounce "place." They usually pronounce the "l" in most words as "r" – like "brouse" for "blouse" or "grad" for "glad," as in "the boy was very grad."

Following the direction given, we walked the first three blocks, as cars zoomed by, honking their horns while petty traders in the streets engaged us with items for sale at what they called, "good deals." Interestingly, or rather confusingly, we passed by several "chop bars." This was a sign that something was wrong with the direction but we did not mind at the time. "Chop bars" were everywhere. Although our friend did not say at what "chop bar" to make the turn, we stopped at every chop bar at every corner and looked to the right, hoping to see if the building we were in search of would be in sight. But it wasn't. Eventually, we stopped after the fifth block, in front of a "chop bar." There, we met another gentleman and inquired of him about the building we were looking for. He was even more specific. He informed us that we had passed our destination and pointed us to exactly where we had come from. He named the streets, told us where to turn and gave us specific landmarks like names of stores on the street. His description was clear and informative, and we were confident it would take us to the destination we were seeking. We walked back the five blocks under the blazing sun, with a bid of frustration over the double walk and waste of time. We came to the street the second gentleman had mentioned to us, and observed that it was the street from which the first gentleman had directed us. We were right back to where we had started when we first asked for direction. I was furious that we had been "played." Oh, how I wished I could see that man again, to confront him about mis-guiding us, but he was long gone. Why couldn't he just say "I don't know"? We couldn't comprehend his actions, but were thankful we finally found what we were searching for.

Over time, we discovered that most Ghanaians we encountered don't know how to say, "I don't know." They pride themselves as a people of knowledge and think it is condescending to say "I don't know." So, they pretend they do know when they really don't. Interestingly, they do so with such conviction that if you have not studied them well, you will believe whatever they say. Hence, what we learned—when it came to seeking information or direction—is how to discern when someone knows from when someone does not. This may not be true for all Ghanaians, but for the ones we interacted with. Our observation proved true each time, especially of the people within the Buduburam-Accra area. They would respond to any question you asked. Whenever you asked any of them a question, this is how you'd know not to believe the answer you get. The answer will begin thus: "Okay"—and the "okay" would be said with a drag— "Okaaay." That then becomes a sign that the person responding does not quite know. So, for me and Solo, "Okaaay" meant: "let me see what I can say about this one" or "I don't know but I will come out with something for you, take it or leave it." We always left it. As a matter of fact, as soon as we heard "Okaaay," we knew the wrong response was coming, and we would try to be polite and say "thank you'" but continue on our journey or move on to another person. For someone who knew the right answer, he/she would say it without giving second thoughts, and particularly, without saying the "okaaay" (let me think). And often when the "non-okaaay" told us something, it was always right. I thought that was one of the memorable moments in my dealings with Ghanaians while in Ghana. So, here is my advice:

if you ever traveled to Ghana and was looking for direction, when you hear "okaaay...," please hit the road running because that person does not know the heck about what you are asking, and if you listen, you will be following a wrong direction.

Lessons Learned: A National Focus

There are two important lessons that I learned from the *Bulk Challenge* experience. I am sharing them with my readers—especially Liberians—with the hope that every individual, every family and every community will take actions to develop attitudes that support and promote peaceful coexistence, opportunities for reconciliation and forgiveness, and a sense of nationalism. It's time to put aside "self" and strive for the common good of all. A national agenda can be developed through instructional modules for inclusion in a national civic education curriculum. The need to teach basic concepts of peace, unity and the value of patriotism in school cannot be over emphasized if we must build communities that ensure the future of our nation riddled with the vices of division, hatred and temptation for destruction. We cannot and must not, and no nation or people should, resort to the imprudence that nearly destroyed the Republic of Liberia.

The first lesson learned:

1) Unity Works: We need one another to survive

Ever since the beginning of time, the idea of needing each other to survive has always been a true phenomenon of life. Although we are overtaken by materialism and the greed for wealth, and are made to believe we are exclusively independent of others, the truth is we do need others. I always knew that, but this *Bulk Challenge* experience actually reinforces my understanding and conviction of the fact that we absolutely need one another to survive. It is no secret that we live in a time when no man is totally, individually complete in all aspects of life. This is in fact, an age-old reality that "no man is an island." Our survival is intrinsically tied to the survival of other people in our families, communities and regions, and even the world. It would be an ill fate to think individual financial status, educational achievement, material wealth, place of birth and parental background are sufficient can make that one individual 100% independent. Whatever and whoever we have become in life, complements who others are, and vice versa. For example, a lawyer needs a doctor, just as a doctor needs an architect, or a banker. The school teacher needs the market woman for food and basic necessities, just as the market woman depends on the teacher to prepare her children for future responsibilities. Everybody needs someone, and in the Liberian case, we have so grown into an interconnected society with mixed or inter-tribal marriages that creating a divide along tribal lines will only cause a wedge that can deepen hurt and strain relationships among us.

Our history has evidence of incidences of tribal conflicts and rivalries leading to long lasting hatred and wounds that need to be mended. The civil war was a culmination of years of built-up hatred, bitterness, tribal conflict, socio-economic disparity, injustices, and demonstrated marginalization of some elements of our society. No doubt, reconciliation is the key to mending the differences and setting the pace for national unity and peace.

The establishment of the Truth and Reconciliation Commission in Liberia is consistent with countries emerging from years of such divisive vices, crises and history of atrocities against individuals and/or groups of individuals. Most, if not all, reconciliation commissions are formulated on the same basic premise: "... investigating human rights violations and abuses; allowing victims the opportunity to tell their story; granting amnesty to perpetrators; and constructing an impartial historical record of the past." However, the specific mandate given to the TRC in Liberia was "to promote national peace, security, unity and reconciliation" by investigating gross human rights violations and violations of humanitarian law, sexual violations, and economic crimes that occurred between January 1979 and October 2003[20]. Under this premise, victims and perpetrators of human rights violations and other forms of abuses are identified and accorded the opportunity to testify to the violations, and request for amnesty. In countries like South Africa, Rwanda, Canada and the Greensboro, TRCs established have helped implement truth and reconciliation that have proved to be successful. For them, implementing recommendations from investigations and other findings was inevitable. Conversely, for Liberia the implementation of recommendations still remains in abeyance. A primary hindrance to the implementation is the fact that some of the findings have adverse effect on the ruling leadership, which came to power after the enactment of the commission. It would therefore be a defeat of the process to implement a part and not the whole of the TRC findings.

What I am saying in short is that truth reconciliation in Liberia has not yet begun, although there are compelling reasons to put events of the past behind us so that we can work toward a stronger and healthier future. We must resolve to implement findings of the TRC so as to break the tribal vices that have eaten up the fabric of our society. Reconciliation must be an ongoing individual and collective process in Liberia, and will require commitment from all those affected. Programs must be developed at all levels to facilitate the continuity of certain processes, such as Students Reconciliation Units in schools and on campuses, or Community Reconciliation Centers in the communities, and Reconciliation Teams in workplaces. Each of these programs should be designed to promote diversity, mitigate issues and resolve conflicts before they escalate into further unmanageable issues. it is important that much effort is put into teaching such learned behaviors as collaboration, partnership, support, teamwork and cooperation; and if we must grow as a nation and make the progress necessary to develop individuals and country, then it is incumbent upon all Liberians to embrace the concept of ONE—we are one— and work together to erase the vices that can destroy our common heritage. Not only is it doable; it is definitely achievable. It has been done by others with much larger diverse groupings, and it can be done by Liberians. We must imprint on our minds that "WE CAN" and we will.

The second lesson learned:

2) Adversity does not discriminate

If we have not already learned, it is important that we understand that adversities, disasters and tragedies do not discriminate. When they hit, the effects are devastating to all, whether the good or the bad, the young or the old, prepared or the unprepared, men or women, boys or girls. Disaster, no matter what form it takes, does not discriminate and leaves no one within its reach, untouched or excluded from its wrath.

I remember very well the 1982 landslide disaster in the mining town of No-Way Camp, in Grand Cape Mount County. When it happened, it claimed the lives of nearly 200 mine workers, and devastated many families, their extended relations and acquaintances, and the entire Liberian populace. It was the first national tragedy of the sort in the 135 years of the nation's history, but as sure as it occurred, it certainly did not discriminate who its victims were. There were men of all categories: fathers, sons, uncles and even a market woman from Monrovia who had gone to No-Way Camp for business purposes. She was swept in the landslide and the only thing found of her was an arm holding onto a handbag with 37 dollars in it.

Like the No-Way Camp landslide, every disaster, the world over, bear similar characteristic of "no-discrimination." The tsunami in Indonesia; yearly California wildfires; the Charleston Church Massacre; the Boston marathon bombing; Sandy Hook Elementary School shooting; the Las Vegas Concert shooting; earth quake in Haiti; Nine-Eleven; plane crashes and other aviation accidents; volcano eruptions in Hawii; Hoko Haram kidnappings in Nigeria; and the shooting at the Jewish synagogue. All of these disasters victimized people of all ages, races, social conditions and economic statuses. With each catastrophic event, the victims were whoever in the vicinity at the time of the havoc.

The Liberian Civil War of 1989 to 2003 was no different. At the onset, it was presumed to be for the ousting of the sitting president. Unfortunately, as it swarmed the nation, over 250,000 men, women, boys, girls, babies and the elderly were killed, and several thousands more went into exile and/or were displaced in foreign nations. The attending consequences of the civil war did not discriminate.

As the *Bulk Challenge* sailed to an uncertain destination, under deplorable and threatening conditions, it didn't matter who each passenger was or where he/she came from; it didn't matter what each person had accomplished or not accomplished; what each person's educational or economic achievement was; we were all connected to a common fate—the probability of drowning in the ocean. There were many times on that boat that we had to collaborate to save our lives. It worked and the lesson to be learned is the understanding that when tragedy hits, everyone is a likely victim. The best way to conceptualize this is to literarily accept the old Liberian adage which says, "Town trap is not for rat alone." I'll help you understand what this means. It's simply saying: when a group of people decides to set a trap in the middle of the city square to catch a frog, not only could it catch a frog but any creeping, crawling and hopping animal that passes in the square. In other words, disaster is like a trap in the city square. You cannot wish it for any particular group of people; because when the disaster strikes, it strikes all within its path and not just the group you wished it for. It will come on all persons: the good and the bad; the rich and the poor; on mansions as well as on the huts; the educated and the illiterates. As a nation and a people, we have had many conflicts that have led us nowhere but the valley of hurt, and grief and pain. It is time that we put aside our egos and work together for the common good of all.

Therefore, the lesson here is, "Never wish for trouble." Do not pray for evil to befall a group of people or wish for an uprising because you do not support a regime or a particular group. If the truth is to be told, our survival or our extinction results from the survival or extinction of individual tribal groups. To every season and purpose, there is time. We must learn to wait for the appropriate time and to take the right actions necessary to address our dissatisfaction, rather than engaging in inimical actions. Because if we do, and it happens, we will not be able to control the extent to which it may escalate, and therefore, we could become victims of our own creation.

TESTIMONIAL

Testimonies are firsthand authentication of a fact[21]. They are assertions of an individual's personal experience and knowledge of a given situation - often made under oath as justification of its truthfulness.

This TESTIMONIAL section came to mind as I compiled my final work for submission to the publisher. I thought it would be phlegmatic to offer the opportunity to other individuals who made that outrageous journey on the Bulk Challenge, to have their voices added to the telling of this story. I was initially hesitant of the reaction I would receive but I reached out anyway, and the response was overwhelming; the encouragement and support for this section was mind-blowing. Each person expressed elation to share in this special opportunity. They were asked to summarize the description of their experiences in response to a single question: "What was the journey like for you on the Bulk Challenge?"

Their responses reminded me of the old Indian folk tale about the six blind men who argued about the description of the elephant although they had never seen an elephant before. According to the story, they argued so much and so adamantly that they were taken to a place where an elephant was and each asked to step up and feel the elephant and describe what they felt. Each blind man feels a different part of the elephant's body, but only one part, such as the side or the tusk. Then they describe the elephant based on their limited experience and their descriptions of the elephant are different from each other, to the point of suspecting that the other person is dishonest[22]. The first blind man reached out and touched the side of the huge animal and described it as a wall; the second blind man put his hand on the elephant's limber trunk and described it as a giant snake; the third blind man felt the elephant's pointed tusk and decided it was a sharp spear; the forth blind man touched one of the elephant's four legs and described it as an extremely large cow; the fifth blind man felt the elephant's giant ear and described it as a huge fan or magic carpet; and the sixth blind man gave a tug on the elephant's coarse tail and described it as a piece of old rope. . "Wall, Snake, Spear, Cow, Fan or Carpet, or Rope!", the truth is, the elephant is a very large animal, and they were all equally right, except that each man had touched only one part of the elephant. And if they were to put the parts together, they would see the whole truth, the bigger picture, and realize that the elephant was more then what they had felt and believed. The moral of the parable or story is that we have a tendency to claim absolute truth based on our limited, subjective experience as we ignore other people's limited, subjective experiences which may be equally true. And if we consolidate our different limited experiences, we will be able to understand beyond our limitation, that things are much more bigger then what we think or know them to be.

So, whether these individuals traveled the entire 10 days' journey to Ghana or disembarked in the Ivory Coast, their testimonies are reflections of the unique experiences and knowledge of each of the individuals – given where they were on the ship and what the conditions and circumstances were within those areas – the summation of which will give us the Big Picture of the experience of the journey. I am therefore, honored to present to you, the testimonies of a few of the people - men, women, boys and girls - who overcame the challenges of Bulk Challenge and the fearful journey. Let their voices be heard!

Eric Collins

"The Bulk Challenge experience was a near-death voyage from hell aboard an overcrowded, sardine-back rusty Cargo Ship destined for Ghana, carrying fleeing Liberian. On board, we ran out of drinking water within hours. There was starvation and sicknesses, no space to sleep, and the terrifying saga of praying in the middle of the Atlantic Ocean for divine intervention to avert the ship's sinking, due to gushing sea water from its hull. The massive excessive weight also endangered us.

Within minutes of paying $75 US dollars and jumping on board, Bulk Challenge was detached from its mooring and began sailing off a day or two ahead of its scheduled departure date. Human movement was nearly impossible, but I managed to advance a foot or two away from the deck railing from where I saw a few persons fall into the water below. My light-frame body was squeezed and swayed to the point of breathlessness.

I was drenched in sweat and seawater from steaming bodies and splashing water and noticed streaks of blood on my arms and clothing obtained from contact with the wounded. As I gain greater consciousness, I noticed all sorts of desperate human conditions around me; like the weak and feeble from undernourishment; those traumatized; and the sick. From there on, I sunk into deeper distress, wondering my own fate and what lies ahead. The hot days and cold nights beat down mercilessly from the open sky onto my sleep-deprived body, leaving burns and scares. My clothes hung loosely on me from the daily loss of body weight. Seldom in 24 hours, scrap of bread or 30ml-60ml (about 2-4 table spoonful) of water was offered by the nearest standing neighbor.

My most terrifying moment on board the dreaded Bulk Challenge experience, and perhaps my most horrifying near-death encounter I ever had, was being alerted early one morning (hours past midnight) that the Ship was taking-in water via a large hole in its hull. Eventually we survived the leak, arrived into hostile neighboring port, and after hours of formality, diplomacy, plead and intervention, we took a short break off high sea. A couple of days later, we arrived to the welcoming hospitality of the Ghanaian people! It was the best thing that had happened to me in months."

Eric Weah Collins
Minneapolis, Minnesota

WEEDOR FAMILY EXPERIENCE:

"Our journey on the Bulk Challenge was not an escape from a civil conflict, but a test of our humanity and perseverance as a people. As horrible as the journey was, it revealed the strength of a people whose confidence and spirit of resilience was solid and unbreakable.

We had to leave our home under the cover of darkness through the assistance of our neighbor; Mr. Vincent Sakifue. That same night, under a heavy tropical rain fall, we reached the Freeport of Monrovia.

We paid for and boarded the Bulk Challenge. We knew little details about the destination of its voyage; we just wanted to leave the City of Monrovia to safety anywhere. In the days that followed its departure, we spent nine terrible, inhumane, sleepless nights and near-death experience on this rusty, unfit cargo ship. The most frightening news was that the ship had a leakage and was taking in water, so much that if it continued, the ship would sink. My wife was four months pregnant, and we thought we were going to lose her pregnancy with no nutritious food, water, medication or a means to determine how she was fairing.

It was a sigh of joy when the ship was allowed to dock at the port of San Pedro in Cote' d'Ivoire' for repairs. The next morning after the repairs was done, we were sent back to high sea to continue our unknown journey.

When we entered the Ghanaian territorial water, we were approached by two Ghanaian navy boats, that fired couples of warning shots to signal the Captain of our ship to come to a halt. At that moment, renewed fear engulfed the ship. Some thought we were being shot at. It was then that we noticed several press camera men on board mini boats approaching the Liberian Refugees ship. They had been following and reporting of the dilapidated conditions on the ship. I believed that prompted the Ghanaian Government to let us into their harbor. Later that afternoon it was announced on a loud speaker, "you are all welcome to Ghana."

It was a relief to know that we would finally get off that ship. It was an experience we have never had before. It was terrible."

Sam & Tenneh. Weedor
Delaware, USA

Kadiatu Konteh-Borajhe

"The journey on the Bulk Challenge was a horrific and traumatic one. I have never been through anything that was so much close to death. During the years of the war, I had many troubling situations – running from place to place for safety. But here we were, on that ship, and on the opened ocean, with no place to run to. Not only that; but we had run out of water and food and medicines. It was a pathetic, horrendous and scary situation. Our fate was death on sea or a miracle of survival. I am glad we overcame those challenging moments.

To this day, each time I think about the journey, I feel disappointed over the lack of cooperation or collaboration amongst African nations. I couldn't fathom the fact that neighboring nations would not have come to the aid of a group of people facing near-death situation. I am not sure how true the information is, but I heard that the Ghanaian Government accepted the ship only after some negotiation with the United Nations. Whether money was paid, I don't know – but not being neighborly until someone else tells you to be, is a sickening thing to know of your neighbors."

Kadiatu Konteh-Borajhe
Riverdale, Maryland, USA

Karmanieh Charlene Reeves

"I was 14 years old at the time, but I still have vivid memories of that journey. We were located in a section that was so cramped with people. There was no space to turn or even sleep. The scent and odor from sweaty bodies around me made me sick to the stomach, but there was nothing I could do about that. I did not spend the entire 10 days of the journey, but the 3 days I spent on the ship can be described as both fearful and as a miracle. I was afraid that a bomb from any of the factions could possibly reach the ship and kill us on board. My greatest fear was when news spread around that the ship could possibly sink because of a crack in it.

All I could think of at that moment was death in the ocean. I was saddened as I thought about school, and friends and all my teachers, and the fact that I would not complete junior high or graduate from high school.

The journey was a miracle because God took us through to Ivory Coast and we (my mom and I) didn't have to get back on board the ship when others did. Mothers with young children, the elderly and pregnant women were taken to a warehouse, where we were given a place to sleep, food to eat, and a good bath. Although I was happy not to get back on the ship, I thought about the thousands of people who had to continue on to Ghana, and couldn't imagine what the rest of the journey was for like for them."

Karmanieh Charlene Reeves
Monrovia, Liberia
Graduated from African Methodist Episcopal University in 2011 with a BA in Sociology

Rev. J. Edwin Lloyd, Sr.

"I was living in the Ivory Coast, in charge of over 400,000 Liberian refugees in Danane. I came to the United States to take my sick sister home to Liberia when the April 6th situation occurred. So, I had to leave on the Bulk Challenge. My plan was to go to Ghana and drive from Ghana to the Ivory Coast – because I knew the ship was heading to Ghana but would not make a stop in the Ivory Coast for just one person.

But the Bulk Challenge was a rotten boat. The voyage was a terrible experience. We were charged to get on that boat, and were beaten by the very Nigerian soldiers who took our money. It was a tussle to get on the boat. One lady's baby nearly fell in the water and we had to help her. I don't know how many thousands of people were on that boat, but it was obvious that it was overloaded. All over the boat was filled with people – from the top to bottom. In addition, it was packed with several cargos – machines, cars, and all sorts of heavy equipment and people's luggage.

We almost sank to the bottom of the ocean. Behold the boat was leaking and they did not tell us. It was supposed to take no more than two to three days to reach Ghana, but after two days, we had not even reached the Ivory Coast yet. Throughout the journey, we prayed and sang songs to help relief the fears. Where God is, there is heaven.

When we landed in San Pedro, I got off the ship to speak with the officials that were on the ground. We met the Minister in Charge of the Refugees. He heard that the boat had trouble and had come to see what the situation was and how he could help. Blessedly, he recognized me and asked, "Is that the Rev. Lloyd? What are you doing here?" I explained, and he said, "You will have to get off that ship." I had some of my children and other people with me.

They pumped the water out of the ship and patched the hole.

The minister left some money with the Police Director that was there and said, "Charter a car for Rev. Lord to go to Danane, but the Officer put me and my crew on a passenger transport and we left.

The leakage of the ship was the main story that made it a difficult journey. It was only God that carried us through."

Rev. Dr. J. Edwin Lloyd, Sr.
Silver Spring, Maryland

Tieh Charles Bropleh

"The voyage on the Bulk Challenge, a vessel not sea worthy, was a nightmare. A 3 day journey took 10 days without food or water. Due to overcrowding, passengers hardly had place to sit or sleep. The terrifying storms during the nights almost drowned us. In this state of despair and hopelessness, Elohim raised up His servants with the Word of God to speak in the lives of the people to bring encouragement, build their faith to trust God and His faithfulness and speak to circumstances and situations to bring them into subjection in the name of Jesus, Phil 2: 10-11.

My takeaway from this ordeal is anyone with the Word of God in his or her heart, and released with faith, can turn any hopeless situation to a hopeful situation, a barren land to fruitful vine, poverty to riches, subdue principalities, expand one territory, etc. Mark 9:23. In other words, no condition is hopeless when Jehovah is in it."

Tieh Charles Bropleh
Monrovia, Liberia

Michel Dioubate, MD

I was a graduating Medical Student at the time of the April 6 renewed fighting in Liberia. Routes for easy escape were limited; the only safe way to leave was by sea and the only ship available was the Bulk Challenge.

In route to the Freeport we stopped by Swedrelief Hospital, and one of the female doctors took us to the pharmacy and gave us some medications to have on us.

The boat owners took seventy-five dollars a person from thousands of desperate people, most of whom did not get on board. For many who made it on board, there was no room or space for them. Close to 4,000 souls cramped aboard this dilapidated cargo ship and the trip was anything but safe.

Our cabin became the clinic and we organized a staff of the three medical students, pharmacy students and volunteers - we were the best they had. It was crowded and filled to capacity day after day, as people stood in long lines seeking care. It was gruesome work and lot of people were sick and weak. A lady reported a guy on the deck near her was immobile and not responding to calls. This university of Liberia student was dead. An older man was worried because his pregnant daughter could not stop vomiting. The Reglan shots did not work as she slowly became more dehydrated. Three attempts failed to put in an IV line and I gave up when my classmate, Joel Jones, found luck after several tries. Another call took me to a cabin where I met the brother of an elementary school classmate. He was having an asthma attack and lucky to get meds I kept for my asthma - it offered him relief. A lady came with a displaced IUD and bleeding and it was scary. It was difficult to even examine her as the clinic was so crowded, somehow God blessed her and she survived the ordeal. Of course, we had ubiquitous cases of dehydration and diarrhea with limited restrooms and exposure to the blazing sun. Hunger and the lack of food was most disheartening part of the experience.

When we disembarked at Takoradi, Ghana, it was almost mid night. We were taken to a school building at Essipon. At the temporary shelter, each refugee was given a mat. After working for two days straight, the only thing I needed was rest. Many people went into the building to find classrooms to sleep or sleep in the halls but I was too exhausted for that. I walked a few steps, put my mat on the grass in the open field and went to sleep immediately.

I stayed to work with Red Cross when they opened a clinic on the Refugee Camp. Months later, after care for the sick, broken hearted and downtrodden, when the hostilities ended, I returned to Liberia.

We were no heroes for doing the right thing when fate put us in the line of duty and service. The true heroes were the Bulk Challengers, the Liberian People and all who bore so well the horrors and nightmares of the war.

Michel Dioubate, MD
New Orleans, Louisiana

Claudia Spiller-Jargbah

"Journey on the Bulk Challenge was a total nightmare. It was horrible, and one like I have never had and pray never to have again. I will never forget the experience. I was on that overcrowded vessel with my mother, husband and children, including my one-year old baby girl. We were clogged up on the opened deck with practically no space to move about. As uncomfortable as it seemed, getting away from the carnage of the crisis was a breadth of relief. We had very little food and water for the journey. My greatest worry was attending to the needs and care of my baby.

One of the children of a lady sitting next to me became sea-sick and vomited on me. It was disgusting, and for the rest of the journey till we disembarked in San Pedro, I stayed in the clothes with the sting of that child's vomit, because there was no privacy and I could not change my clothes.

Although I was overtaken with fear when we heard that the ship could possible sink, my faith was unshakable. I knew if nothing else, God will make a way for us. So, it was elating when the ship docked at the port in San Pedro for repair work. There, I got off the ship with my mother and children. Unfortunately, my husband – like all other men – were not allowed to get off the ship – partly because of the rumors that rebels were on the ship. We were taken to a warehouse and given blankets, buckets, soap and towel, and food. For the first time in three days, I took a bath, ate some food and slept a restful sleep. It was a blessing to get off that ship."

Claudia Spiller-Jargbah
Philadelphia, Pennsylvania

Dr. Pearl Banks-Williams

"The journey was terrible. There were lots of anxiety; too many people for the boat, and the uncertainties were just indescribable. We did not know when the boat was leaving. Every day we were told it will leave tomorrow; and it seems like tomorrow never came. So, the suspense of not knowing when we were leaving created all the anxiety. And then we finally got on board but had no clue how long the journey would take. It was our first time traveling by sea – my husband, our 3 years old son and I. We were just excited that at least we were leaving all that shooting and fighting behind.

About 30 minutes into the journey, the boat came to a standstill. After a while, we saw a tug boat come by with some prominent government officials and former warlords. They got on, and the ship continued the journey. The bath rooms were down in the cabins and you had to fight your way through the crowd to go down just to ease yourself. Someone came up from the cabin and informed us that the ship had problem; that it was leaking and taking in water. The news created fear and panic on the ship.

My husband worked for UNICEF at the time; so, when we landed in San Pedro, we were among those who traveled by road through the Ivory Coast to Ghana.

In a nut shed, the journey was traumatic and hopeless. Had we taken our time and asked the relevant questions, we probably would not have gotten on that ship in the first place.

Pearl Banks-Williams, PhD.
President, International School, Liberia

Hon. Gayah Fahnbulleh

What a journey! Is all I can join my many compatriots to say
about the sinking Bulk Challenge ship to Ghana. It was the most
distasteful and nauseating journey ever in the lives of Liberians. It
was disgusting, sickening, horrifying and dehumanizing; but God
was in controlled and by His mercy and divine grace, we survived
the journey.

I was a vocal and outspoken member of the Liberian National
Legislature, against Charles Taylor, his thugs and their criminal
operations, at the time of this fracas. My life and that of my family
were easy targets. The ECOMOG Commanding General, John
Mark Ineigar, recognized that and sent a military escort to take me
and my family to the ECOMOG Headquarters.

Few days later, General Ineigar informed me that a ship called
the "Bulk Challenge" was planning to leave Liberia for the Ivory
Coast, Ghana and/or Nigeria. I believed the cost of the ticket may
have been either $50.00 or $75.00 per person. I managed to
purchase tickets for my family and several others who were
desirous of leaving the country but did not have money.

I was taken to the Captain who gave me one of the most
luxurious suites on the ship. But when the news of water gushing
into the ship was revealed, there was nothing luxurious about that
suite. Fear set in and each day was marked by anxiety, extreme
apprehensions and nervousness that something bad was going to
happen to us.

One day Charles Taylor got on BBC and made careless and
reckless utterances that everyone on the ship were rebels. This led
to hesitation of the government of the Ivory Coast to allow the ship
in its port. Though his pronouncement was incorrect, he was also
not totally wrong either. There were some members of defunct
Warring Factions on the ship.

I vividly recalled a gentleman informing the group that the
Captain wanted a prominent Liberian to counter Taylor's arrogant

assertions on the BBC and other News Outlets that the ship was carrying only rebels. I also remembered a former member of a defunct warring faction, elected to take on the task. This angered many of the University students, men and women on the ship; they took serious exception with him - claiming that if he spoke, he would seriously jeopardize the safety of everyone on the ship and also justified Mr. Taylor's emphatic statements. They were so mad, they threatened to throw him and the others into the ocean, but peace subsequently prevailed as there were emotional appeals from all persuasions for their safety. In no time, few Liberians recognized me and requested that I take the mantle, which I immediately did and was escorted at once to the Captain's office. I introduced myself and took the radio and spoke to the BBC - rebutting Taylor's assertions, on behalf of Liberians and the hundreds of Voyagers.

In the days that followed, The BULK CHALLENGE became more challenging. People became sea sick and there were little or no medication on board the ship to treat them. As we got closer to the Ivorian borders, they refused us entry into their territorial waters. The Captain tried several times as we appealed to them, but to no avail. The Ivorian authorities finally allowed the BULK CHALLENGE to dock on humanitarian grounds, to repair the ship. Other International interventions had them to acquiesce for women and children to get off to drive to Ghana.

I was also offered this opportunity to go along with my family to Ghana by land, but because of my role as spokesperson, a leader of the people, I returned on the ship, like the others, and continued the journey – although with high skepticism of undependability of this sinking ship.

Several persons died on the journey, as I recall; one person, very close to where I was. The dead body remained for a couple of days before it was taken downstairs and thrown into the ocean.

Indeed, the journey was one I will never forget, but one that surely demonstrated a spirit of unity and love amongst Liberians – a total opposite of what was going on in our country. I saw people caring for one another; for those they did not even know; strangers took care of strangers; giving away food and wears; nursing and encouraging one another to get well soon. Though we face a harsh today and maybe a bitter tomorrow, I see hope that one day, Liberians would rise above their indifferences to move that nation into greatness.

Gayah Fahnbulleh
Gaithersburg, Montgomery Co.
Maryland

Prince Jemel-Yarmah Jallabah

The experience on the Bulk Challenge was rough, to say the least; but God took us through and we finally landed in Ghana. I did not have the money to pay for the journey; so I forced my way through a window of the ship and landed in the bathroom. Immediately, I was struck me in my eye. I felt the sharp pain run to my head. For a moment my vision was blurred. I could barely see a thing. I started to cry.

I was glad to be leaving the fighting behind, but I had no clue where the ship was going. My joy was short lived, and fear set in when we learned that the ship was not sea-worthy. My spirit sank. I was drained. I was confused. I was disappointed. I prayed for divine intervention.

The scariest moment for me was the night it stormed. The ship started to lean to the side as if to capsize. My heart started to pound; like you're about to die but you can do nothing to help yourself. Then a lady raised a song, and we all joined in and started to sing. It seemed the Holy Spirit took control; the storm calmed down; the ship was balanced again; and we went through the night without any serious incidence.

Prince Jemel-Yarmah Jallabah
Correction Officer/Columbus, Ohio

Alston Wolo

"The journey on the Bulk Challenge in 1996 was terrible. It was an adventure I will never forget. Running from the fear of the fighting in the city, we were confronted with the fear of death on the ocean – especially, after we learned that the ship was leaking.

Thankfully, we land in Abidjan – San Pedro – to have some repair work done on the ship. What a relief it was. Some Ivoirians came to the port yard with food and water and threw them over board into the ship. The Ivoirian authorities also showed some curtesy to women and children by taking them off the ship and to a warehouse where they were given a bath, change of clothes and food. After the repair work was complete, we got back on the ship although we did not want to, but we also could not stay in the Ivory Coast either. Unfortunately, the authorities were under the impression that we were all rebels.

Many people got sea-sick on the ship including my wife who had diarrhea; and with no water, food or medication, it was a frightening situation. I didn't know what to do or think. Thankfully, the late Dr. Joel Jones and Dr. Mitchell Teobatti had some medicine and helped my wife and she regained her strength and the diarrhea stopped. When we landed in Ghana, two bodies were taken off the ship.

Alston Wolo
Providence, Rhode Island

Feona Muabon Johnson-Togba

The journey on Bulk Challenge was a terrifying experience. The fierce fighting in Monrovia started on my birthday - April 6th – one reason I will never forget this time. We were blessed to get on board the ship - myself and my three children. It was distressing even to get on the ship. Everybody wanted to go but couldn't. There were so many people – much more than the ship could hold. So, for us to have gotten on was a blessing. When the ship sailed off, I felt a sense of relief and safety – getting away from the horror of the fighting.

But when word spread that the ship was taking in water, and that it could possibly sink, I felt even more terrified that my children and I were going to perish in the ocean. I could not swim; and even if I could, how would I have managed with three children. So, when the ship docked at San Petro for repair, I was so elated that the authorities took down mothers and children and carried us to a warehouse.

Authorities of the United Nations and other Non-Governmental Organizations made arrangements with the Ivoirian Government to grant permission for their staff and family to be transported to Ghana by road. The rest of us were to return to the ship for continuation of the journey. I was not mentally prepared to get back on that ship with my children knowing what I knew about it; not even after the repair work. So, I started to cry profusely, that an old friend of mine decided to take my children and I with him and his fiancé to Ghana as part of his family."

Feona Muabon Johnson-Togba
Hamilton, Canada

Theophylus During, II

"Traveling on the Bulk Challenge was a terrible moment for me. Although we had paid to enter the ship, we were denied entry when it was time to board the ship. I had to struggle to make my way on the ship; trading off my bracelet, watch and chain to a soldier to allow me on the ship. I was fortunate to have been located in one of the cabins on the ship. It was small and could accommodate no more than four persons. An ECOMOG Captain was also in that section with me and carrying five (5) vehicles from Liberia to Nigeria.

Because of my activeness and curiosity, I moved around a lot and befriended some of the working men on the ship, and sometimes operated with them like a crewman. One night, I was with the crewmen and we discovered that the ship was leaking and that water had entered a good portion of the harsh. They were afraid at what they saw and decided they would put on their life jackets and jump into the ocean and swim away before anything catastrophic happened. The captain had to talk them against their plans, noting, it would cause more panic on the ship and perhaps lead to more deaths if the people found out what and why they were swimming off. So they decided to stay on board and work with the Captain's plan to get the ship to San Pedro in the Ivory Coast.

At San Pedro, the repair team pumped out several gallons of water from 7am to almost 6pm – nearly eleven hours. We were not allowed to get off the ship because Charles Taylor had announced on the BBC that all the young people on the ship were rebels. So, although there was no guarantee as to the durability of the repair work, there was no option to stay in the Ivory Coast. We had to leave.

There was an old man who died on the ship from cholera. Many persons did not know. After he died, we had to wrap him up in a thick white blanket and had him kept somewhere no one could notice easily. We traveled with that dead body till we arrived in Ghana."

Theophylus During, II
Junior Transport Officer, LRA - Liberia
Graduated from University of Liberia in 2013 with a BA in Sociology

C. Wilfred Williams

The journey on Bulk Challenge was a bitter-sweet experience: good and bad. Good in the sense that we got out of Liberia at a crucial time when it was dangerous; especially, when you consider that many people at the port wanted to leave but couldn't, because they did not have any money. Other people 'stole-their-way' on the ship, while some bribed their way into the ship till it was overcrowded.

It was our first experience on a ship, and Bulk Challenge had its own challenges; no food, no water and no medicine.

Just before we entered the Ivorian territorial waters, we learned that the ship was leaking. It was fearful news, but we made it into the port, by prayers and the grace of God. After we docked at San Pedro, the men were told to remain on the ship for fear of news earlier in the day which reported that we were all rebels on the ship. The Ivorian authorities took our wives and children away, and after repair work was done on the ship, we continued on to Ghana

As horrifying and traumatic as the journey was, I was glad we left; because after we returned to Liberia, we were met with the news that some of our friends who had remained in Liberia at the time of the ship's departure, had died during the very April 6th fighting in Monrovia.

C. Wilfred Williams
Deputy Director General
Internal Audit Agency, Republic of Liberia

Grant Martin

Bulk Challenge was an interesting experience. I had no plans to leave the country. I was just passing around and heard that a ship was at the Freeport and was leaving with Liberians.

Earlier, I had gone to see my mother, and while there, she explained how my little sister had cried all through the night and stating that she couldn't stand the war.

So, I took my little sister and we went to the Freeport. The area was packed with lots of people, trying to leave the country. The Nigerian soldiers were beating people as they tried to get on the ship. Even those who paid could not enter the ship. Neither my sister nor I had ticket for the ship. I just hustle our way on the ship and was glad we made it without paying a dime. When the ship took off, everyone was jubilant – hopeful of getting to a war-free country soon. The ship was over crowded. I visited the lower areas of the ship where the cargo was kept; and I observed that water had entered the ship to the point of covering some of the cars that were in the hatch. But I didn't think much of it until later, when rumor spread that the ship might sink.

The ship was refused entry to the Ivory Coast, except for some repair work in San Pedro. The Ghanaian Government also refused the ship but eventually allowed the ship to dock in Takoradi, and we were taken to Assepon and later to Senzule, where the UNHCR established a refugee camp for us.

Grant Martin
Stockbridge, Georgia

Fatu Barduae

I was a privileged passenger on the Bulk Challenge, because of my sister who had a son for the man who had chartered the ship – Tom. My mother and all my siblings were part of my entourage and we were located in the staging area within the ship. There in that area, also were Gayah Fahnbulleh, James Davis, and Mario Hoff. But the journey was no good at all.

From Liberia to Ghana, it was a horrible trip. People were getting sick each and every day. Some medical students and doctors (Mitchell and the late Joel Jones) tried to help as best as they could with the few medicines and first aid items they had but that didn't last. I heard that a boy died of TB. I also saw a man who sat on the engine died; probably from the heat, and I believed they threw him overboard into the ocean.

One night my sister came to me and said that the ship was leaking; and that the captain was seeking approval from nearby countries to allow them to fix the problem. Soon after I heard the news of the leak, Charles Taylor made a pronouncement that the ship was filled with rebels and that no country should accept it. I was immediately overtaken with fear – because I knew if we didn't stop to fix the problem the ship could possibly sink. Although the ship was not filled with just rebel, it was true that people like Tom Woweyue and some other factional leaders were on the ship. One of them volunteered to be the spokesperson for the passengers. He wanted to respond to what Charles Taylor had said, but some men on the ship protested and insisted that they could not speak. They further threatened to throw them overboard into the ocean, but other people intervened on their behalf.

The people of San Pedro were nice to us. They brought us food; and allowed the women and children to get off the ship and were taken to a warehouse. After the ship was repaired, we continued to Ghana. At first, the Ghanaian government refused to accept us, but they later allowed the ship to dock in Takoradi.

We survived the journey by the grace of God. Although there was no food, the fear of death took away the apatite. I survived on drinking just water and little food stuff that people shared. Many people were kind enough to share with their neighbors, whatever little they had.

Fatu Barduae
Randallstown, Maryland

I am thankful to each one of these individuals for sharing their experiences, and presenting in a way, a broader perspective of the journey. What is true and common to all of us, is the fact of the experience – it was fearful, horrifying and traumatic. But much more than that, each of us is a testament to the spirit of resilience and fortitude, and the ability to persevere - the manifestation of which is seen in how each person overcame the trauma of this journey, to become what we have made of ourselves: teachers, doctors, lawyers, business men and women, great moms and dads, community leaders, and the like. This, for me, affirms the fact that situations in life do not have to define us; that it is not what life hits us with that matters, but rather, what we do in and beyond those situations. Those are the moments and circumstances that make us.

This is the story of the experience of the Bulk Challenge.

References / Bibliography

[1] **AIESEC** | Live the experience *aiesec.org*

[22] An ancient and well known fable from India https://**www.peacecorps.gov**/.../resources/story-**blind-men**-and-**elephant**

[19] Anonymous

[5] Carter Camp Massacre; Massacres in Liberia's Civil War – an internet publication of massacres during the Liberian Civil War – Monday, March 26, 2007

[13] Chicago Tribune - REFUGEE FREIGHTER STILL SEEKS REFUGE *https://www.chicagotribune.com/news/ct-xpm-1996-05-13-9605130166-story.html*

[6] Cow Field Massacre on Duport Road. News Newspaper, December 19, 1994 Vol. 5 # 151

[7] *Freeport of Monrovia*: **NPA: National Port Authority of Liberia** www.npaliberia.com/operations/monrovia

[16] *Ghana Web - www.ghanaweb.com/*(Takoridi) All about Ghana: business, culture, education, government, latest news and background information.

[17] *Ghana Web - www.ghanaweb.com/* (Essipon) All about Ghana: business, culture, education, government, latest news and background information.

[18] *Ghana Web - www.ghanaweb.com/* (Buduburum)
All about Ghana: business, culture, education, government, latest news and background information.

[14] Hank Hanegraaff, Magic – October 2013 – Crystalinks
www.crystalinks.com/Magic.html

[9] J.F. Kennedy - http://www.oceanofnews.com/15-sea-quotes/

[15] Lady Abigail, The Glass Witch Magick Shoppe. Copyright 2013
http://www.theglasswitchmagickshoppe.com

[8] LBDI – Liberian Bank for Development and Investment
http://lbdi.net/

[4] *LIBERIA*: **Government and rebels sign** *peace agreement* **Irin**
www.irinnews.org/.../l iberia-government-and-rebels-sign-peace-agr...
IRIN, ACCRA, 18 August 2003 (IRIN) -

[21] Merriem-Webster Distionary: Definition of testimony

[12] MSF medicin san frontierers, Home | Doctors Without Borders -
USA *https://www.doctorswithoutborders.org/*

[1] *Peace Agreements: Liberia* – **Peace Agreements Digital Collection
| by the United States Institute of Peace**
www.usip.org/.../peace-agreements-liberia

[2] *Peace Agreements: Liberia* – **Peace Agreements Digital Collection
| by the United States Institute of Peace**
www.usip.org/.../peace-agreements-liberia

[3] *Peace Agreements: Liberia – Peace Agreements Digital Collection | by the United States Institute of Peace*
www.usip.org/.../peace-agreements-liberia

[10] **San**-Pédro (Côte **d'Ivoire**) - Britannica.com
www.britannica.com/place/San-Pedro-Cote-dIvoire

[20] United States Institute of Peace
https://www.usip.org/publications/2006/02/truth-commission-liberia

BBC News - *Liberia* country profile - Overview
www.bbc.co.uk/news/world-africa-13729504

Ghana Refuses to Take In a Boatload of Liberian Refugees - New ...
www.nytimes.com/.../ghana-refuses-to-take-in-a-bo...

About the Author

Ezax Smith is a native of Liberia, West Africa, and author of "Pillars of Life". He holds a Bachelor of Science (BSc) degree in Economics and Accounting from the University of Liberia, and a Master of Science (MS) degree in Non Profit Management, from Eastern University, Pennsylvania. He also completed graduate studies in Education at the Coppin State University in Baltimore, Maryland.

Ezax has done extensive work with young people – in the church and community – as a Youth Counselor, Coordinator, Resource Person, Program Developer, and Teacher. In 1998, he founded HOPE For Tomorrow, Inc. – a local non governmental organization (NGO), to help train disadvantaged young people, coming from the devastation of the Civil War in Liberia. He is a former high school teacher with the Baltimore City Public School System and former Adjunct Faculty at the Baltimore City Community College (BCCC). Currently, he is the Training Coordinator at the Institute of Professional Practice, Inc. (IPPI)/ Mid Atlantic Human Services Corp.

He has received several awards including the 2006 Educational Service Award, from the Maryland State Department of Pretrial and Correctional Services; Outstanding Teacher Award in 2009, from the Baltimore City Public School System; the 2011 Baltimore Mayor's Award for Exemplary Leadership in Baltimore, and the 2013 recognition for leadership in Education by Liberian Awards, Inc.

A former president of the Liberian Association of Maryland (LAM), he is a Christian, married to Madia Bengue-Smith, and their union is blessed with four children and four lovely grandchildren.

CPSIA information can be obtained
at www.ICGtesting.com
Printed in the USA
LVHW041739200620
658099LV00006B/455